HOLY WHOREDOM

HOW THE MODERN PRIESTS OF BAAL AND ASHTORETH ARE TURNING OUT THE DAUGHTERS OF ZION TO HARLOTRY

By Believer X

Have You Not Read Press

Holy Whoredom

Copyright © 2010 by Believer X, ISBN 978-0-578-05932-7
All rights reserved solely by the author. The author guarantees all contents are original and do not infringe upon the legal rights of any other person or work. No part of this book may be reproduced in any form without the permission of the author.

Believer X's Blog:
www.believerx.wordpress.com

Scripture quotations marked (NASB) are taken from the NEW AMERICAN STANDARD BIBLE®, Copyright ©1960, 1962, 1963, 1968,1971,1972,1973,1975,1977,1995 by The Lockman Foundation. Used by permission.

Scripture quotations marked (CEV) are from the Contemporary English Version Copyright © 1991, 1992, 1995 by American Bible Society, Used by Permission.

Scripture quotations marked (NLT) are taken from the Holy Bible, New Living Translation, copyright 1996, 2004. Used by permission of Tyndale House Publishers, Inc., Wheaton, Illinois 60189. All rights reserved.

Scripture quotations marked (YLT) are from Young's Literal Translation Public Domain.

Scripture quotations marked (NKJV) are taken from the New King James Version. Copyright © 1982 by Thomas Nelson, Inc. Used by permission. All rights reserved.

Scripture quotations marked (ESV) are taken from English Standard Version" The "ESV"; and "English Standard Version" are trademarks of Good News Publishers.

Scripture quotations marked (NIV) are taken from the HOLY BIBLE, NEW INTERNATIONAL VERSION®. Copyright © 1973, 1978, 1984 Biblica. Used by permission of Zondervan. All rights reserved.

The New Testament Greek Lexicon based on Thayer's and Smith's Bible Dictionary plus others; this is keyed to the large Kittel and the "Theological Dictionary of the New Testament." These files are public domain.

NAS Exhaustive Concordance of the Bible with Hebrew-Aramaic and Greek Dictionaries. Copyright © 1981, 1998 by The Lockman Foundation. All rights reserved. http://www.lockman.org/.

Cover image, Devil dressed in a business suit © courtesy of James Thew Used with permission. Cover image, Devil woman with bone pitchfork © courtesy of AlienCat Used with permission. Cover image, Priester 4 © courtesy of Honeyfee Used with permission.

Ezekiel 43:6-12 NASB

Then I heard one *speaking to me from* the house, while a man was standing beside me.

He said to me, "Son of man, this is the place of **My throne** and the place of the soles of My feet, where I will dwell among the sons of Israel forever **And the house of Israel will not again defile** <u>My holy name</u>, neither they nor their kings, by their harlotry and by the corpses of their kings when they die,

by setting *their* threshold by **My** threshold and *their door post beside* **My** *door post,* with **only** the wall between Me and them. **And ...**

they have defiled My holy name by their abominations which they have committed. So I have consumed them in My anger. "Now let them put away their harlotry...

...and the corpses of their kings far from Me;
and I will dwell among them forever.

"As for you, son of man, describe the temple to the house of Israel, **that they may be ashamed of their iniquities;** and let them measure the plan.

"**If they are ashamed...**

of all that they have done...,

<u>make known to them</u> the design of the house, its structure, its exits, its entrances, all its designs, all its statutes, and all its laws And write it in their sight, so that they may observe its whole design and all its statutes and do them.

"This is the law of the house: its entire area on the top of the mountain all around **shall be most holy.**

Behold,
this is the law of the house.

This book is dedicated to the only person that is truly deserving of a dedication, my only TRUE friend in this world, M. French. Until we met not long ago, I was living out this prophecy of scripture in a very real way for many years:

Psalm 142 NASB

Prayer for Help in Trouble

Maskil of David, when he was in the cave. A Prayer.
I cry aloud with my voice to the LORD;
I make supplication with my voice to the LORD.
I pour out my complaint before Him;
declare my trouble before Him.
When my spirit was overwhelmed within me,
You knew my path
In the way where I walk
They have hidden a trap for me.
Look to the right and see;
For there is no one who regards me;
There is no escape for me;
No one cares for my soul...

Without her in my life to talk to and encourage me over the last year I do not know if I could have endured much more loss. Thank you dear woman of God, for helping me to stand and for holding up my arms when I became weary in the battle. Thank you for your effort in all of the selfless contributions you made in the cover art and the editing of this book, as well as being the inspiration to even write it. You shall not lose your reward.

Believer X

TABLE OF CONTENTS

FOREWARD	7
PREFACE	10
INTRODUCTION	17
1. Defining Marriage	32
2. What Makes A Covenant?	44
3. Adultery/Fornication	60
4. Genuine Righteousness	75
5. Sound and Not So Sound Doctrine	89
6. The Circumcision	105
7. The "church" or THE CHURCH	122
8. Judgment, Recompense, and Vengeance	134
9. Sordid Gain	158
10. The Adulteress, The Harlot	167
11. Putting a Pin in It	183

FOREWARD

I can assure you that this book will be well worth your time, and will be like nothing that you have ever read before. However, be prepared to be challenged, it will make you uncomfortable and you will probably be offended. That is the intention of this book. You should be offended and disgusted by the shameful behavior in a "church" that looks no different than the world. If it walks like a duck, if it quacks like a duck...CAN IT BE ANYTHING ELSE? You should be offended by the immorality surrounding (and leavening) you. We need to start using righteous judgment and stop judging by appearances, and start calling evil what it is... evil, and start calling good...good. Jesus called a hypocrite a hypocrite. He would call a duck...a duck.

Scripture is only profitable if it comes with reproof. This book is full of reproof, but the reproof is coming directly from another book, your Bible. Most people have no problem believing that all of the great promises and the warm fuzzy verses in God's Word are speaking to them, but He is reproving us throughout His Word as well - yes, YOU and me.

So, I hope you will humble yourself and "receive with meekness the engrafted word that is able to save your soul." If you aren't prepared to go to the cross, die to self, and say, "Father, not my will, YOUR will be done," then there is no point in reading further.

I was shocked when I began studying God's Word just a few years ago, because it was in such contradiction to anything being taught in the "church" today. I couldn't believe what a mockery and perversion was being made of the institution of marriage even within the church, when God takes it so seriously that He made it an earthly illustration of His covenant with us. I was dumbfounded to discover how much divorce was sugarcoated and embraced in the church, when God clearly states that **He HATES it.**

Holy Whoredom

Why doesn't the church hate what God hates? They have no problem calling homosexuality an abomination. Why doesn't the church hate all of these broken homes for children who have "christian parents"? Is there even such a thing as an irreconcilable born again believer, and two people living according to biblical principles who cannot live at peace with one another?

Didn't God gives us the ministry of RECONCILIATION? Where is the "love" that never fails and endures all things? Jesus said, "By this, they will know you are my disciples…**by your LOVE."** One of the most obvious things that struck me right away, was that **divorce goes against all that Christ represents**…but the church can't even see this hypocrisy.

Jesus raised the bar so high in the Sermon on the Mount, that it can only be done in the supernatural, but the church continues to lower its standards, which are a far cry from biblical standards. We are called to respond in the exact opposite manner of the world- that's what sets us apart. But no one is actually called to **"love their enemies"** and **"forgive seventy times seven"**, and **"not repay evil for evil."** It's OK to hate your enemy, not forgive, and cast stones if your spouse is an adulterer, or if they do just about anything that makes you not like them anymore.

What happened to, **"Husbands, love your wives the way Christ loves the church?"**

Husbands are abandoning their families, and being told they are *forgiven* (without truly repenting), because *God knows we all fall short, and He loves and forgives us no matter what.* I guess they haven't read Malachi 2. If that is their picture of Christ, then they should be showing their spouse the same understanding and mercy. There is no such thing as **"for better, for worse…til death"** anymore. No one is actually expected to be "Christlike."

Paul said a steward of God's mysteries must be found **faithful.** How many divorced or remarried Pastors are there? Most of the others at least give hearty approval. The author of this book has proven himself faithful in the midst of extreme treachery on many levels, by his own wife and family. His only motivation for writing this is to reach people with the truth, to open their blind eyes, and to get them off of the broad road that leads to destruction.

He will not say things that tickle your ears, like God warns us that the false teachers will. This book will never be a bestseller...it isn't supposed to be. If you hate the message that you are about to read, that is a good indicator that it's the truth. Jesus said He would be hated by all men, and that we would be hated as well for proclaiming His truths.

You might find the language in this book too harsh, and it probably won't be "politically correct" in your circles, but God doesn't refrain from calling someone what they are:

Proverbs 12:1 NASB

"Whoever loves discipline loves knowledge, But he who hates reproof is **stupid**."

Proverbs 1:7 NASB

"The fear of the LORD is the beginning of knowledge; **Fools** despise wisdom and instruction."

None of us wants to be called a stupid fool by God one day in the presence of all, so I hope you will be wise and heed the warnings that follow.

M. French

PREFACE

This book is the result of a lifetime spent in the quest for THE TRUTH. Contrary to what many believe, Truth is not something that is easily obtained. Only God is the sole administrator of Truth, and Jesus made it clear in His preaching that only the truth can set you free. **But you must know it.** That means someone has to tell you. **"How will they hear unless someone is sent?"** Jesus sends His apostles to those in desperate need of His message.

I will be writing this book in the style of me speaking *(ARIAL typeface)* directly to YOU. This is how **APOSTOLIC (one that is sent by Christ) WISDOM** is communicated. So if you are fearful of reading something that will make you extremely uncomfortable, and almost certainly angry, you might as well put this book on the shelf.

I will occasionally be using words from the original texts to make things clear where the English language is imprecise. Do not let this intimidate you. It is solely for your benefit and isn't for the purpose of me putting myself above you intellectually. I am your servant in this regard because I have studied these things.

Here is the first example. That word **know** in John 8 is one of several Greek words (15 in fact) found in the Greek scriptures that are all translated into a single grouping of English words for *know, known, knowledge, and unknown.* So merely reading an English Bible will put you at an immediate disadvantage if you are only willing to believe what lying Bible translators and your wicked pastor tells you. It means to understand something by taking in knowledge, through one's mental faculties. It is differentiated from another Greek word that means to know in a much deeper way. This is another word that is used to indicate a full knowledge.

So in this instance in John 8, Jesus was talking about an abstract, basic kind of knowing, in the same way that you can know that 2+2=4. But He also talks about **experiencing or knowing** God's mysteries that are not available to those who reject the basics of simple cognitive understanding.

That is the main perspective of this book, one of simply knowing and understanding basic truth regarding marriage and adultery as it is defined by God alone, through the testimony of His son Jesus Christ and His apostles.

I will not burden you with an overabundance of these detailed explanations, but I do want you to get a sense of what you are missing by using the English Bible as your sole reference for determining what is true. There are many easy to use resources available to anyone, that can simply read English.

I do not claim any special education, I just read English myself, so I would recommend that you consider doing your own research to verify anything that I say.

If **knowing truth** is primarily a function of the intellect, then it can be assumed that it should be devoid of any emotional constraints or sensually motivated biases. For me truth is like math. I don't care how passionate or emotional you are, you will never be able to convince me that 2 apples plus 2 apples does not EQUAL 4 APPLES. God set up the universe to be governed by the laws of physics, most of which are unseen - but transgress the law of gravity by walking off of a cliff, *just once,* and you will assuredly FEEL the penalty of disregarding that immutable law.

God's spiritual laws are no different in their severity to those who so cavalierly dismiss His truth on any number of subjects, including this one. But there are those who would lead you to believe that "the blood of Jesus" applied mystically at some point in your distant past absolves you of any real consequence of perpetual sin.

That is one notion you will have to **divorce yourself from**, if you will accept the truth found on the pages here. If that were true (Jesus' blood constantly excusing YOUR CONTINUED SINFUL LIFESTYLE), there would not be so many verses to the contrary.

Holy Whoredom

Warning people about their sin and rebellion is the principle task of God's elect. The scripture also makes it clear that God's people will not only reject the message, they will also treat the messenger in the precise manner that Jesus told them not to.

That is been the story of my existence for most of my adult life. As a relatively young man I had what can only be described as a heavenly vision, not unlike the one Saul of Tarsus experienced on the road to Damascus in Acts 9, and similar to Ezekiel's vision in Ezekiel 1. That was over 20 years ago, and as a young naive individual, I made the tragic assumption that the Lord would be present among christians and in the churches where I thought, based on their sincere assertions, **"The Word Of God is believed, taught, and obeyed here." EMPTY TALK!**

Well, I never fit in for very long anywhere that I went even though I was initially hailed as a prophet at each church I attended. My first pastor Jerry Bryant (an adulterer himself) and his whore of a wife Cindy, knew the late Keith Green and they would often compare me to him - saying with a hint of derision, **"You are just like Keith!"** when I wouldn't compromise and they were none too pleased with my pronouncements. Well, that lasted for about one year. Then I was no longer a great prophet, suddenly I was a know-nothing punk, when I quoted the letter to the church at Pergamos from Revelation 2 to Jerry and Cindy concerning their unbiblical practices and standards.

So I went from church to church trying to find someone who could identify with what the Lord had revealed to me. I was either seriously wronged and left on my own or asked to leave. When I left or was booted from any church, I did my best to maintain a civil tone with former members and leadership. I thought that is what Jesus would have me to do. I was still blind to all of the deep wickedness permeating the American church. But I persevered, looking, seeking, yet not obtaining. There was a restless disappointment that was setting in - **why is there no zeal for even the simplest of Christ's commands?**

I didn't learn much from preachers or books and tapes, even though I devoured many christian resources, attended conferences and showed up whenever the doors opened.

Believer X

After years of hearing 2-3 *"life-changing"* sermons per week, and not actually seeing people nor myself really change, it got tiresome and I pitched the whole mess as I saw it. I thought to myself, **"Someday the Lord will bring me into something amazing."** I knew He had shown me His glory that night where I experienced His Love and inexplicable Holiness - the memory of that has never departed from me throughout all the years and hardships I have endured at the hands of wicked, God-hating christians.

At first, I thought most christians and the worthless shepherds who led them, were only moderately deceived, and that with a little effort and God working, we would be able to come to the Truth eventually. But alas, that wasn't in the cards that God had already ordained for me. He caused me to suffer even more rejection and pain for the very purpose of opening *my* blinded eyes AND covering *my* nakedness.

Recently, it has only intensified and made my life more miserable, because of the truth He led me to discover, that I will be sharing in this book. But truth is precious. God does not give it to those that will trample it underfoot. Nobody believes they are wrong, but with over six billion people on earth with so many different views, somebody (most in fact) must be. This holds true in christianity... with so many opinions, but no solid agreement on this and many other issues.

If God does give you truth, He will also cause you to suffer because of it. Do you believe that you have the truth? What have you lost for the sake of it? I have lost everything for the truth. That is not to say that just because one suffers, that they will obtain truth or that they already possess it. Many people suffer in many ways, but you must suffer in the manner which is outlined in scripture, in order to make any legitimate claim that you have Gods validation/approval. That is exactly what has occurred to me - I find myself fulfilling scripture after scripture in the circumstances of my life. It is the only way you can practically **make your calling and election sure.**

American christianity is so far removed from any resemblance to the reality of what the Bible teaches.

So I know that most people, who somehow find themselves reading this book, will not be able to accept it, because they are so entrenched in their traditions and the reassuring comfort of the **FALSE** majority opinions. I am used to it, but I do it anyway because I am compelled to.

So, if you are divorced, contemplating it, or already remarried, you are the one who really needs to take this to heart, and not casually dismiss it based on your prejudice, that is mainly influenced by your emotional/sensual desires. You have to deny yourself and lose your life if you will ever find it. I have lost mine, and I hope this book will open the eyes of your understanding to grasp what is really a **kindergarten level course in God's kingdom**.

If you receive the truth contained in this book, you will open the door for God to bring you even greater treasure. Sadly though, if you wish to maintain your unbiblical positions surrounding this teaching, **you can only expect to receive a far greater condemnation and harsher judgment than even those who prostrate themselves before sticks and rocks!**

Peace,
BelieverX

FOR THE PURPOSE OF DISTINGUISHING ORIGIN:

I will be quoting THE SCRIPTURES in THIS (Times New Roman). ***BLACK* and *RED*** (in the E-Book version) Typeface – I will also insert scriptural words and phrases in the text of my writing (in Blue Arial) using this type as well.

chRIsTiAn IdIoTs are designated by THIS (COMIC SANS MS) TYPEFACE.

Ezekiel 2:1-5 NASB

Then... He said to me,

"Son of man, stand on your feet that I may speak with you!"

As He spoke to me the Spirit entered me and set me on my feet; and I heard Him speaking to me.

THEN... He said to me,

"Son of man, I am sending you to the sons of Israel,

to a rebellious people who have rebelled against Me;

they and their fathers have transgressed against Me to this very day.

**"I am sending you to them

who are stubborn
and obstinate children,
and you shall say to them,
'Thus says
the Lord GOD.'

"As for them,
whether they listen or not-
- for they are
a rebellious house -

they will know
that a PROPHET
has been among
them."

INTRODUCTION

PROVERBS 30:5-6

NLT

Every word of God proves true.
He is a shield to all who come to him for protection.
Do not add to his words,
or he may rebuke you and expose you as a liar.

CEV

Everything
Everything
Everything
God says is true-
and it's a shield for all
who come to him for safety.
Don't change what God has said!
He will correct you and
show that you are a liar.

NASB

Every word of God is tested;
He is a shield to those who take refuge in Him.
Do not add to His words.
OR...
He will reprove you, **AND you will be proved a liar!!!**

Ecclesiastes 1:9-11 NASB
**That which has been is that which will be,
And that which has been done is that which will be done.**
So there is nothing new under the sun.
Is there anything of which one might say,
"See this, it is new"?
Already it has existed for ages
Which were before us.
There is **no remembrance** of earlier things;
And also of the later things which will occur,
There will be for them **no remembrance**
Among those who will come later still.

Ecclesiastes 1:9-11 NLT
History merely repeats itself. It has all been done before.
Nothing under the sun is truly new.
Sometimes people say, "Here is something new!"
But actually it is old; nothing is ever truly new.
We don't remember
what happened in the past, and in future generations,
no one will remember what we are doing now.

NOW THIS:

Titus 1:10-11 NASB
For there are **many rebellious men,
empty talkers, and deceivers,**
especially those of the circumcision,
who must be silenced BECAUSE they are upsetting
(LIT. *subverting, overturning, tearing apart*) whole families,
**teaching things they should not teach
for the sake of sordid gain.** One of themselves, a
prophet of their own, said, "Cretans are always liars, evil beasts,
lazy gluttons." This testimony is true. **For this reason...**

(What reason? **DESTROYING FAMILIES!**)

...reprove them severely

so that they may be sound in the faith, not paying attention to **Jewish myths** and commandments of men who **turn away from the truth.**

Since **every Word of GOD is tested**, I will be highlighting and enlarging ones that I want you to carefully consider, that you may have overlooked previously when reading the Bible. I will also be using a complement of translations that faithfully bring out the meaning of certain highlighted words within the text. This has taken me many years and I have never made a penny from my study of the scriptures. I did it only for the purpose of obtaining truth. It was God that put this hunger for the truth in me.

Ecclesiastes 1:9-11 is a foundational truth that must be applied to everything else we read in scripture - spiritual principles transcend any historical or dispensational mindset. Don't you think God is clever enough to bring about the same basic spiritual, invisible realities, with an infinite number of historical scenarios and circumstances, with *just* enough variation in order for your pride and arrogance to blind you to the absolute recurring **truth in every generation of Ecclesiastes 1:9-11?**

I assure you that He can!

Matthew 23:29 NASB

"Woe to you, scribes and Pharisees, hypocrites! For you build the tombs of the prophets and adorn the monuments of the righteous, and say, **'If we had been living** in the days of our fathers, **we would not have been partners with them in shedding the blood of the prophets.'"**

"IF WE WERE AROUND BACK THEN, KNOWING WHAT WE KNOW NOW, WE WOULD NOT HAVE BEEN STUPID ENOUGH TO KILL GOD'S CHOSEN MESSENGERS."

OH...really? **WELL, THEY KILLED THE MOST PROLIFIC AND TRUTHFUL OF ALL OF GOD'S MESSENGERS! HIS SON JESUS CHRIST!**

This is that very principle in action, and to whom it applies...**Blind leaders** who think that they have learned from the mistakes of the past. But that is not what God says. He says **there will be no remembrance.** That mentality is the byproduct of spiritual blindness, compounded by arrogance. The truth is veiled from those who are proud. I've passed through my **proud, miserable, poor, blind, and naked** phase. I wasted over thirty years by spinning my wheels in the lies of mainstream christianity, which is **TOTALLY DEVOID OF GOD'S TRUTH ON EVERYTHING!**

For about 1,000 years, the vile roman whore kept THE Word of God from the masses, but now since we have a overabundance of Bibles available to us, that could no longer be possible, right? I mean really, everyone has access to the Word of God, right? Nope, sorry genius, God says **what has been, is that which will be...**and then He says this:

Jeremiah 8:7-9 NASB
"Even the stork in the sky Knows her seasons; And the turtledove and the swift and the thrush. Observe the time of their migration;
But **MY** people <u>*do not know!*</u> The ordinance of the LORD. "*How can YOU say*, 'We are wise,
And the law of the LORD is with us'?
But behold, <u>the lying pen</u> of the scribes
HAS MADE IT INTO A LIE... INTO A LIE ...
INTO A LIE... INTO A LIE... INTO A LIE...
"The wise men are put to shame,
They are dismayed and caught; **Behold, they have rejected the word of the LORD,**

And what kind of wisdom do they have?"

Again: That which has been...
IS THAT WHICH WILL BE!

So logic dictates, that if the scribes (seminary trained, EVIL Bible translators of today) **make God's Word into a lie** as it says, then it follows that people will be misled, yes? A lie's only purpose is to deceive and God ordained it.

THE SCRIPTURE CANNOT BE BROKEN!!!

So they (the scribes) can accomplish the same essential result that the roman catholic abomination brought about, all the while making most people like you arrogantly think:

"If I had been alive...in the dark ages I would have _____ " (fill in the blank).

Well, I have got a news flash for you, **Nicodemus,** you are in the dark ages RIGHT NOW! The truth of the scriptures is just as hidden from you as any miserable serf that attended mass, paid indulgences for his dead relatives in order to get them out of the NON-EXSISTENT flames of purgatory, and was unable to read Latin. You are just **IN BONDAGE** to a different set **OF MYTHS**!

NOW, I am no "scholar," but it doesn't take a rocket scientist to see something is amiss, with so many translations and opinions as to what they (the scriptures) all mean. I have looked at the original languages with only my own common sense, powers of observation, deductive reasoning, AND God's Spirit to tell me where to look. But I have come up with a completely different conclusion on the real meaning of the scriptures.

Just like **Elijah and Michaijah** during the period when wicked Ahab and his idolatrous wife Jezebel ran Israel and oppressed the people, **I stand alone against the overwhelming majority of false prophets that claim to speak for Jehovah.**

Hmmm...tolerating Jezebel?
NOTHING NEW!

Jezebel had been dead about 1,000 years when she was referenced in Revelation 2, but she was called by name.

Holy Whoredom

Was this a literal woman who had the sad misfortune of being given the name of one of the most vile women in the Bible? Or could Jezebel be representative of a reality that no one recognizes, or will even begrudgingly acknowledge in themselves? Well, if Jesus told the Laodocians they DID NOT KNOW THEY were blind, then Jezebel would also be able to go unnoticed there, too.

NOTHING NEW...
NOTHING NEW...
NOTHING NEW...
NOTHING!
and NO REMEMBRANCE!

Remember these scriptures, because I will be repeatedly referring to them. In addition to the verses in Ecclesiastes 1 and Titus 1 as the main premise of this book, I would add that these are ALWAYS APPLICABLE to God's Word:

Sanctify them in the truth, Thy word is truth. John 17:17
The sum (all of) Thy word is truth. Psalm 119:160
The scripture **cannot** be broken. John 10:35
Thy commandment is **EXCEEDINGLY BROAD**. Psalm 119:96

So, does Ecclesiastes 1:9-11 **HAVE ANY** application to Titus 1:10-14? I don't believe anyone in the church thinks what Paul was addressing in Titus 1 is relevant any longer, because they think that literal circumcision is a dead issue. But those in the circumcision have never really left the church as an ongoing spiritual reality. **They are the ones in power... JUST LIKE JESUS SAID THE PHARISEES WERE IN HIS DAY.**

Now, you don't have to force men into actually cutting off their foreskins (most have it done to them as babies anyway) in order to fall under the principles of the following texts and translations of Titus 1:10-14.

NLT
For there are **many rebellious people** who engage in **useless talk** and deceive others. This is especially true of those who insist on circumcision for salvation. They must be silenced, because they are turning whole families away from the truth by their false teaching. And they do it **only for money**. Even one of their own men, a prophet from Crete, has said about them, "The people of Crete are all liars, **cruel animals**, and lazy gluttons." This is true. So **reprimand them sternly** to make them strong in the faith. They must stop listening to **Jewish myths** and the commands of people who have turned away from the truth.

CEV
There are many who don't respect authority (of God's Word), and they fool others by **talking nonsense.** This is especially true of some Jewish followers. But you **must make them be quiet. They are after money, and they upset whole families by teaching what they should not.** It is like one of their own prophets once said, "The people of Crete <u>always</u> **tell lies. They are greedy and lazy like <u>wild animals</u>.**" That surely is a true saying. And

you should be hard on such people...

(this command makes men pleasers cringe)

...so you can help them grow stronger in their faith...

Being mean just for the sake of being mean, isn't why I do this. It is so people will turn from their unmitigated hostility toward God. This is what authentic preachers and heralds are pressed into service to do. It is the plight of the second son that says, *"There is no way I am going to work in your vineyard Father and face those treacherous men you left in charge all by myself."* I know full well my words will not be received by the masses or the wicked shepherds and false apostles that lead them in rebellion against God's holy commands.

Holy Whoredom

...Don't pay any attention to any of those **senseless Jewish stories** and human commands. **These are <u>made up</u> by people who won't obey the truth**.

YLT
For there are many both insubordinate, vain-talkers, and mind-deceivers -- especially they of the circumcision -- whose mouth it behoveth to stop, who whole households do **overturn**, teaching what things it behoveth not, for filthy lucre's sake. A certain one of them, a prophet of their own, said -- `Cretans! **always liars**, evil beasts, lazy bellies!' This testimony is true; for which cause **convict them sharply,** that they may be sound in the faith, not giving heed to **Jewish fables** and commands of men, turning themselves away from the truth.

ESV
For there are **many** who are insubordinate, **empty talkers and deceivers, especially those of the circumcision party**. They must be silenced, since they are **<u>upsetting</u>** whole families by teaching for shameful gain what they ought not to teach. One of the Cretans, a prophet of their own, said, "Cretans are always liars, evil beasts, lazy gluttons." This testimony is true. Therefore **rebuke them sharply,** that they may be sound in the faith, not devoting themselves to **Jewish myths** and the commands of people who turn away from the truth.

If we are commanded to be **DOERS OF THE WORD, NOT MERELY HEARERS, THAT DECEIVE THEMSELVES,** why doesn't anybody take it upon themselves to obey this command? Mainly, because there are so few who **have received a love of the truth**. That is what this book is about - doing the thing no one else seems to have the cajones to do - identifying who the circumcision is and **reproving them harshly** with the the **truth of God's Word:**

There is not any statement made by God that can make any other statement made by God untrue.

That would in effect make God A LIAR.

OBSERVE:

Sanctify them in the truth, Thy word is truth. John 17:17
The sum (all of) Thy word is truth. Psalm 119:160
The scripture **cannot** be broken. John 10:35
Thy commandment is **EXCEEDINGLY BROAD.** Psalm 119:96

Christian leaders and pastors somehow think that they can peruse the expansive buffet of God's Word and pick the things they desire to eat, and ignore the rest to their own shame, while at the same time they are doing a great disservice to the people who believe that they hold all the answers. Well, they don't! They are **liars and rebels** in the light of the clear teaching of scripture and the passage gives the reason - **SORDID GAIN**! What would be the outcome if the biblical standards regarding **divorce and remarriage being in fact adultery** were taught, strictly adhered to, and obeyed?

I will tell you what would happen to those massive ministries and mega churches. People would leave faster than rats on a sinking ship, because the truth is, a large percentage of christian adults are **committing real sexual sin by being remarried** and the rest of those congregations extend them the hand of fellowship thereby disobeying the command **to avoid the irreconcilable (2 Tim 2:3-5)** and the command **not to associate with sexually immoral so-called brothers (1 Cor 5:9-11)**.

Now what would be the economic fallout of everybody leaving churches in droves because they are rightly **accused of adultery,** or are **tolerating it by their associations**, and are **unwilling to stop their whoring and stop giving hearty approval?**

WHO IS GOING TO PAY ALL THOSE UNSCRIPTURAL TITHES AND MANIPULATED OFFERINGS THAT KEEP THE WICKED MACHINE OF THE CHURCH, THAT DESTROYS FAMILIES, IN OPERATION? <u>**NO ONE!**</u>

Why are there books like this written about divorce and remarriage with three and even four different views in them?

Divorce-Remarriage-Four-Christian-Views

Holy Whoredom

I mean really, what is the sense in debating a topic that has such far reaching implications on the certainty of this one doctrine and then not coming to any substantial conclusion? There is no argument among christians about the truth of this statement:

1 Corinthians 6:9-10 NASB

Or do you not know that **the unrighteous will not inherit the kingdom of God? Do not be deceived;** neither fornicators, nor idolaters, **nor adulterers,** nor effeminate, nor homosexuals, nor thieves, nor the covetous, nor drunkards, nor revilers, nor swindlers, **will inherit the kingdom of God.**

If you want to know if remarriage is or isn't adultery, you can simply read a book and let the Holy Spirit be your guide. *Since everyone just adores Christ, and christians can't do anything other than please Him, there will be no problem with them falling into line with God's Word!* What a crock! Christians hate God - they demonstrate their unbridled wickedness by their continual rejection of truth. Their disagreement and debating over this simple issue without any resolution, is evidence that they do not possess the Spirit Of Truth!

The commands of Christ will bring any TRUE BELIEVER to the place of isolation from the values of the world among those who:

"HONOR ME WITH THEIR LIPS, BUT THEIR HEART IS FAR FROM ME"

and those who:

"CALL ME LORD, AND DO NOT DO AS I SAY!"

But no one in the church thinks they are actually guilty of anything. That is an unscriptural and very **DANGEROUS** position to hold. The New Testament was written to people who said they believed in Christ, but it is chocked full of accusatory statements, reproof, and indictments aimed directly at them!

1 Corinthians 6:8 NASB
YOU wrong and YOU defraud -
AND THAT **YOUR BROTHERS!**

(How? By using the GODLESS COURT SYSTEM, which is unequivocally prohibited!)

JAMES 4 NASB

YOU LUST, **YOU** COMMIT MURDER, **YOU** ARE ENVIOUS, **YOU** FIGHT, AND *(YOU)* QUARREL, **YOU** ASK WITH WRONG MOTIVES, SO THAT **YOU** MAY SPEND IT ON **YOUR** PLEASURES...

7-YOUS! *In just 2 little verses!*

YOU YOU YOU YOU YOU YOU YOU !!!

Then this:

YOU ADULTERESSES!

YOU COMMIT MURDER!!!

ARE CHRISTIANS COMMITTING MURDER??!!

Of course they are:

THE SCRIPTURE CANNOT BE BROKEN!

SO, WHOMEVER JAMES WAS WRITING TO: James 1:1 THE 12 TRIBES, WAS GUILTY OF **MURDER,** but the concept OF **MURDER** is just as **invisible** to the **blind leaders** and the clueless sheep that hearken to their lies, as the reality of there still being a **circumcision party ruling the earthly Jerusalem** (Galatians 4:21-25). They will keep you under the **oppressive yoke of sin** by telling you that **"no one can be totally sinless."** This is what Jude was talking about - false teachers **turning the grace of God into licentiousness** *(lit. unbridled lust)*.

Now, can God's true grace really be turned into licentiousness? or is that phrase in Jude 6 really a metaphor saying that they (false teachers) will tell you that grace is something it really isn't, such as **"*unmerited favor*"?** Grace has far more meaning than the narrow terminology that lying clergy assign it. Peter calls it **manifold grace.** Paul said, **"grace teaches** (or more accurately) **chastens us to deny ungodliness and worldly desires and to live sensibly, righteously, and godly in this present age!"** (Titus 2:12)

YOU...tolerate Jezebel and she teaches my bond-servants...

to do every manner of evil. SHE

teaches and leads My bond-servants *astray* so that they commit acts of WHORING and eat things sacrificed to idols...she does not want to repent of her WHORING...Behold, I will throw...those who commit ADULTERY with her into great tribulation, *unless* they repent of <u>her deeds</u>...the deep things of Satan.

Now, do I think very many people will repent of *her* deeds? No, not really, scripture doesn't teach that very many will even **receive a love of the truth.**

Even fewer will be able to communicate it properly. But most believe that the smorgasbord available in christianity has something for everyone, and that **sound doctrine** is not actually singular, but it can be found within the multitude of diverse opinions about anything and everything biblical.

That is just nonsensical delusion.

Here is a prime example concerning the departure from **sound doctrine** within the whore church. John Calvin - Jacob Arminius, who is right, who is wrong? Whose teaching **is fitting for SOUND DOCTRINE?**

Predestination or freewill? Why don't christian ministries, publishers, and bookstores that recommend both, see their own duplicity?

Here are the possibilities:

A. Calvin - true teacher, Arminius - false teacher
B. Calvin - false teacher, Arminius - true teacher
C. Calvin - false teacher, Arminius - false teacher

I know the answer is C, *they are both false teachers,* but most christians think the correct answer is:
D. none of the above, Calvin - true teacher, Arminius - true teacher, and that you can have **massive error** and still be approved by God... **PREPOSTEROUS!**

By recommending both Calvin and Arminius, ministries are asserting that they are both true teachers. That is an intellectual impossibility, because their teachings are diametrically opposed to one another.

Now most ministers in their little secret exclusive club will not get overly hostile with each other and **"agree to disagree"** covering their **cowardice** with a **thin slimy layer of whitewash** under the guise of **"christian love"**.

When Paul came on the scene approximately 20 years after Jesus was raised, he got right in Peter's face and said Peter was **under condemnation** for doing something as seemingly insignificant as **not eating with Gentiles**. We have leaders taking their stance on polar extremes of this issue, but when they are done with their debate, they slap each other on the back, shake hands, and say something as insipid as:

"Well, I guess we will know when we get to heaven".

What happened to:

John 14:26 NASB
But the Helper, the Holy Spirit, whom the Father will send in My name, He will teach you ALL things, and bring to your remembrance all that I said to you.

OR:

John 16:13 NASB

But when He, the Spirit of truth, comes, He will guide you into all the truth.

Christianity has had nearly 2000 years and they cannot come to any definitive TRUTH? Well, not in the false gospel you won't. I believe the apostles went to their graves with ALL THE TRUTH and every other generation has had the few that persevered and came into all truth, and they were treated shamefully, just like every other true messenger of God has ever been treated throughout the ages.

Matthew 23:33-35 NASB

YOU serpents, YOU brood of vipers, how will YOU escape the sentence of hell? "Therefore, behold, I am sending YOU *prophets* **(AND APOSTLES- Luke 11:49)** and *wise men* and *scribes*; some of them YOU will kill and crucify, and some of them YOU will scourge in your synagogues, and persecute from city to city, so that upon YOU may fall the guilt of all the righteous blood shed on earth, from the blood of righteous Abel to the blood of Zechariah,the son of Berechiah, whom YOU YOU YOU YOU YOU YOU YOU MURDERED between the temple and the altar.

So are there any true servants like the ones described above, faithfully teaching God's unyielding precepts? I do believe there are, but I have yet to meet a single one. Scripture bears this principle out with Elijah's situation - even though God said He reserved 7,000 for Himself, Elijah thought there wasn't anybody else, based on his own experience.

Likewise, even though I've searched the land, I haven't encountered any true teachers in person or on TV - since anybody like me would not have the audience required to sustain a show, because it's about money!

So, ditch your preconceived ideas, your emotional biases, and all of the meaningless arguments you have ever been led to accept, and let's begin to look at what the scriptures actually say! Here is a partial list of the things I will cover:

Marriage, covenant/bound, adultery, fornication, righteousness, sound doctrine, the circumcision, wrath, love, judgment/ recompense/vengeance, salvation, faithfulness/vows/idle words, treachery, sordid gain, overturning families, true repentance, earthly/heavenly church, empty talk, leaven, unrighteous courts, authority, warning, innocent party, exception clause, gender specific accountability, nothing new, the many/the few,

and most importantly...
EVERY WORD OF GOD IS TESTED.

There are hundreds of things you literally don't know. I am not kidding, so I can only cram so much information into this brief book. But, if you begin with the premise and are **truly ashamed at all of the abominable acts that you have done,** I will be able to show you **the law of the house**.

Which is...
THE LAW OF CHRIST!

Chapter 1
Defining Marriage

Hebrews 13:4 NASB

"Marriage is to be held in honor among all, and the marriage bed is to be *undefiled;* for fornicators (whoremongers - KJV) and **adulterers God will judge.**"

Since this book is about marriage and what constitutes a holy marital bond, we have to define terms as they are outlined in the scriptures. Now, marriage is not a word that holds any specific denotation. Even in the Bible, it has primarily two different categories - holy and unholy. Jesus used the word **marries or weds** to designate PARTICIPATION in a ceremony where vows are exchanged, and He called those who married outside the parameters of God's strict holy ordinances, adulterers and adulteresses, whores and whore-mongers. He acknowledges the reality of **a union recognized ONLY by men** when He said:

Luke 16:18 NASB

EVERYONE who divorces his wife
and marries another...

He said this in the context of this statement in verse 15:

And He said to them, "You are those who justify yourselves in the sight of men, **but God knows your hearts;** for that which is highly esteemed **(an illicit marriage?)** among men is detestable (KJV - an abomination) in the sight of God...

Believer X

> **...EVERYONE** who divorces his wife and *marries* another **commits adultery,** and he who *marries* one who is divorced from a husband **commits adultery.**

What Jesus *did* specify, was how God views it's respective participants in relation to it's validity in His eyes. In a world that allows you to change sexual partners as frequently as soiled underwear, marriage in American culture has little to no value, despite what holier than thou, Bible-thumping christians want to assert about its sanctity:

"It is only designed between a man and a woman, God made Adam and Eve, not Adam and Steve, an abomination," blah blah blah...

I will prove those statements contain more HYPOCRISY than a Klansman claiming the Lordship of Christ, while he gleefully strings up somebody of a darker skin color.

Now, what the world may call marriage, is commonly accepted by the church, as long as it is between a man and a woman. Well, as our culture sinks lower and lower into depravity, the church of salt and light is supposed to stem the tide of wickedness. But are they really salt? Are they really light? Let's look at this pragmatically from the scriptures.

Christians argue that allowing sodomites to wed will somehow devalue the God created institution of marriage. They spend their resources and energy fighting against it, when in fact they continually ignore the words of the very **ONE** whom they say that they represent. I am not in any way advocating same sex unions, that is not what this book is about.

What I am saying, is that the whore church is so hypocritical in it's tone, that they will be judged far more severely than the most flamboyant homosexuals, because they **nullify God's commands** concerning marriage for the sake of their meaningless arguments, **traditions,** and allowances concerning MDR... (**M**arriage/**D**ivorce/**R**emarriage).

Hebrews 13:4 NASB
Marriage is to be **held in honor** among all, and the marriage bed is to be **undefiled;** for fornicators and **adulterers God will judge.**

This may be a good time to do a little clarification of terms. Let's look at the word **fornicators** or in the KJV **whore-mongers**. Its root word noun (fornication, fornicate – v.) is an old English word that has pretty much fallen out of its proper use and connotation. It has broad meaning and application in the Bible and it's meant to convey something **exceedingly unclean** and odious to God. **Fornication** is accurate, but I prefer *whoring*. It is more forceful in its impact upon the reader.

I will also use the words "fucking" and "screwing" to emphasize the vileness of the act, because they are just words - they are not sinful - they are descriptive of **defiling sins**. When I use them, it is not for the purpose of arousing one's prurient interest, it is to awaken the reader or listener to its offensiveness. It is unlawful illicit sexual relations. It is offensive to God and the one who is victimized by it, **so get over typed words** on a page.

God doesn't shy away from using descriptive AND GRAPHIC SEXUAL language concerning **whoring and adultery**, but the liars that translate the Bible for the stupid sheep that venerate them by calling them **"godly"** and **"scholars"** are fearful of offending the precious sensibilities of their audience - after all, the main purpose is to sell overpriced Bibles. What christian is going to buy a Bible with the word "fucking" in it?

Let's take one passage from several translations and see how they all seem to water down some words, while keeping others intact:

Ezekiel 23:18-20 NIV
When she carried on her **prostitution** openly and exposed her nakedness, I turned away from her in disgust, just as I had turned away from her sister. Yet she became **more and more promiscuous** as she recalled the days of her youth, when she was a prostitute in Egypt. There she lusted after her lovers, whose **genitals were like those of donkeys and whose emission was like that of horses.**

NLT

In the same way, I became disgusted with Oholibah and rejected her, just as I had rejected her sister, because she flaunted herself before them and gave herself to satisfy their lusts. Yet she turned to **even greater prostitution**, remembering her youth when she was a prostitute in Egypt. She lusted after lovers with **genitals as large as a donkey's and emissions like those of a horse.**

KJV

So she discovered **her whoredoms,** and discovered her nakedness: then my mind was alienated from her, like as my mind was alienated from her sister. Yet she **multiplied her whoredoms,** in calling to remembrance the days of her youth, wherein she had **played the harlot** in the land of Egypt. For she doted upon their paramours, **whose flesh is as the flesh of asses, and whose issue is like the issue of horses.**

YLT

And she **revealeth her whoredoms,** And she **revealeth her nakedness,** And alienated is My soul from off her, As alienated was My soul from off her sister. And she **multiplieth her whoredoms,** To remember the days of her youth, **When she went a-whoring** in the land of Egypt. And she doteth on their paramours, **Whose flesh [is] the flesh of asses, And the issue of horses -- their issue.**

ESV

When she carried on her whoring so openly and flaunted her nakedness, I turned in disgust from her, as I had turned in disgust from her sister. **Yet she increased her whoring,** remembering the days of her youth, when **she played the whore** in the land of Egypt and lusted after her paramours there, **whose members were like those of donkeys, and whose issue was like that of horses.**

Why so much disparity in these terms? You have words for **prostitution or whoring** (in the Hebrew culture this word did not always mean an exchange of money was an essential aspect of the act), which have been sanitized and evolved in polite society as the word **"fornication"** and even worse, **"immorality"**. Now, immoral is a generic term, meaning anything unrighteous or wrong - even pagans use it. At its base that is true, because God uses the term **fornication or whoring** to signify anything that takes His place as the only One to be worshiped.

Holy Whoredom

When Jezebel teaches the bond-servants of Christ to commit acts of fornication in Revelation 2, that is talking about false worship of pagan deities and yet it is exposed...IN THE CHURCH!

What church? The true church? Or is there another church you have yet to discover? Just wait, let's not get ahead ourselves.

You also have phrases regarding men's genitals and seminal ejaculations resembling that of large farm animals! God is much more angered by people refraining from using the offensive and suggestive language He originally meant to convey, than He is of me using a contemporary term like *fuck,* for the purpose of evoking an INTENDED visceral reaction of disgust.

You should be disgusted. God wants you to be disgusted by shameful wicked behavior.

Read a few verses down in Jeremiah 8, from where I previously quoted - **it ends with a telling indictment:**

Jeremiah 8:10-12   NASB

Because from the least even to the greatest

Everyone is greedy for gain;

From the prophet even to the priest

Everyone practices deceit.

"They heal the brokenness of the daughter of My people superficially, Saying, 'Peace, peace,' But there is no peace.

"Were they ashamed because of the abomination they had done?

THEY CERTAINLY WERE NOT ASHAMED, AND THEY DID NOT KNOW HOW TO BLUSH."

Believer X

Look at all the similarities between Titus 1, Luke 16, Ezekiel 43, and these 2 passages in Jeremiah - **abomination, greedy, deception, ashamed, wickedness.**

Jeremiah 6:7-15 NASB

For thus says the LORD of hosts, "Cut down her trees and cast up a siege against Jerusalem. This is the city to be punished, in whose midst there is **ONLY OPPRESSION.** "
As a well keeps its waters fresh,
SO SHE KEEPS FRESH HER WICKEDNESS.
VIOLENCE AND DESTRUCTION ARE HEARD IN HER;
Sickness and wounds are ever before Me.
 "Be warned, O Jerusalem, Or I shall be alienated from you,
 AND MAKE YOU A DESOLATION, A LAND NOT INHABITED."
Thus says the LORD of hosts, "They will thoroughly glean as the vine the remnant of Israel;
 Pass your hand again like a grape gatherer over the branches."
To whom shall I speak and give warning that they may hear? Behold, their ears are closed and they cannot listen. Behold, the WORD OF THE LORD HAS BECOME A REPROACH TO THEM; **THEY HAVE NO DELIGHT IN IT**.
But I am full of the wrath of the LORD;
 I am weary with holding it in
"Pour it out on the children in the street and on the gathering of young men together; For both husband and wife shall be taken, The aged and the very old. "Their houses shall be turned over to others, Their fields and their wives together;
For I will stretch out My hand against the inhabitants of the land," declares the LORD.
 "For from the least of them even to the greatest of them,
EVERYONE IS GREEDY FOR GAIN,
And from the prophet even to the priest.
EVERYONE DEALS FALSELY.
"They have healed the brokenness of My people superficially,Saying, 'Peace, peace,' But there is no peace.
"Were they ashamed **because of the abomination they have done?**

They were not even ashamed at all; They did not even know how to blush.
Therefore they shall fall among those who fall; **At the time that I punish them, They shall be cast down," says the LORD.**

Now, it says **EVERYONE** in several places, but that cannot possibly be directed at the christian church, "the body of Christ."

"That *must* be talking about those dirty stupid Jews in the old testament! We are God's chosen people now until Jesus returns to graft those evil Jews (who rejected their Messiah and had Him killed) back into the olive tree."

"All scripture is given by inspiration, and is **ONLY** profitable for doctrine" **Right?**

What does it say?
REPROOF! CORRECTION!! TRAINING IN RIGHTEOUSNESS!!!

Maybe my use of colorful language will teach you **HOW TO BLUSH AND BE ASHAMED** of the **ABOMINATIONS** you have been indifferent to all of these years. Paul said he spoke things to "the shame of his readers," but apparently *THEY WERE NOT ASHAMED*.

Tiger Woods is a Buddhist, and he was ashamed of his whoring. He wouldn't even allow himself to be seen in public for three months. But christians divorce, remarry, and carry on their **shameful behavior** in front of the whole community **without any appearance of sorrow or guilt,** because there are no Apostles permitted to call them out and **make them ashamed**!

The reason for the lack of clarity and uniformity is that **they (translators - scribes) are all liars.** They cannot even think clearly, because they are under the influence of **THEIR DEMONIC DOCTRINAL BIASES**, instead of God's Spirit.

I will further prove this as we proceed.

So, the "church" gets all self-righteous about the detestable gays wanting to legalize their unholy relationships, primarily to feel validated as people, and take advantage of the benefits allotted to married couples. I don't give a rip about what pagans do. They are going to sin and do vile unnatural acts to one another whether they marry or not, but here is something you may never have considered before:

Romans 1:18 NASB
For the **wrath of God** is revealed from heaven against **all ungodliness** and unrighteousness of men who **SUPPRESS THE TRUTH IN UNRIGHTEOUSNESS**...

Now skip down to verse 26 that fundamentalist evangelicals just love to quote condemning homosexuality:

...for this reason God gave them over to degrading passions; for their women exchanged the natural function for that which is unnatural, and in the same way also the men abandoned the natural function of the woman and burned in their desire toward one another, men with men committing indecent acts and receiving in their own persons the due penalty of their error.

"How wicked and vile those perverse queers are!!!"

Well, you need to bite down on that **blasphemous piece of meat that is wagging uncontrollably in your mouth** because in just 1...2...3...4...verses we read this little nugget:

...without understanding, **UNTRUSTWORTHY**, unloving, unmerciful...

HERE IS ONE OF THE MANY EXAMPLES WHERE THE LIARS WHO TRANSLATED YOUR BIBLE HAVE INTENTIONALLY LED YOU ASTRAY.

That word **"untrustworthy"** is far more complex than the English language can convey in a single word. It is so packed with meaning, yet it is largely ignored by almost all preachers (yours truly being the sole exception). I didn't learn this stuff from men, it came by the **unveiling of Christ within me**.

Holy Whoredom

God says that those **untrustworthy people are under His wrath as much as those homos** in verse 27, AND those who give **"hearty approval" are just as guilty before God**. What is **hearty approval**? More on that later...

So, what is that word **"untrustworthy"** actually talking about?

Definition from Vines NT dictionary:
GR. Asunthetos - from suntithemi (lit- to put together) with the neg, prefix *a*, hence 'not covenant-keeping' i.e., **REFUSING TO ABIDE BY COVENANTS MADE!!!**

Now, who does that sound like...hmmm???, **covenant-breaking, faithless!** "Asunthetos" also has an equivalent meaning in the Hebrew scriptures by way of the Septuagint, where it is used to denote treachery here:

Jeremiah 3:8-11 NASB
And I saw that for all the **adulteries** of **faithless** Israel,
I had sent her away and given her a writ of **divorce**,
yet her **_TREACHEROUS_** sister Judah did not fear;
but she went and was a harlot **(went whoring)** also.
"Because of the lightness of her harlotry, she polluted the land
and **committed adultery with stones and trees.**
"Yet in spite of all this her **_TREACHEROUS_** sister Judah did not return to Me with all her heart, but rather in deception," declares the LORD.
And the LORD said to me, "Faithless Israel has proved herself more righteous than **_TREACHEROUS_** Judah."

The key point here is, that **asunthetos** presumes an initial state of peace, evolving into that of unrighteous betrayal (divorce), followed by a continued state of hostility, which those without mercy refuse to end peacefully. It is a description, at the very heart, of an irreconcilable unilateral, no-fault divorce.

How many wedding ceremonies have you attended where there are standard vows like:

TO LOVE AND CHERISH
TO HONOR
TO OBEY (FOR THE WOMAN)
I still don't get how the unbridled rebellion of contentious whores is applauded in the church. My favorite Jezebel is Joyce Meyer, what a **VILE, UN-GODLY WOMAN!**
IN SICKNESS (BODILY OR MENTAL?)
FOR POORER
FOR WORSE (or just for "BETTER")
Would this include: *beatings, abandonment, adultery*?

What does the word **"worse"** mean, if it doesn't imply hardship, even from your spouse? There is a Pauline concession that I will discuss later for a spouse who is being physically abused to separate, but it does not nullify the covenant that is still binding until death. <u>Stay with me, I'm not advocating staying with someone who is beating you, but it is no justification for divorce either.</u>

UNTIL DEATH DO US PART...hah!

How about this little phrase that is only a meaningless repetition at nearly every wedding:
"Is there anyone here who knows any reason why these two cannot be joined according to scripture?"

What if someone said, "Yeah, I know of about 100 verses in scripture why this isn't Holy". How about someone actually quoting Luke 16:18 at the wedding of a **treacherous, divorced whore or whore-monger who left their covenant spouse?**

Not bloody likely, because the very **whoring churches** and **wicked shepherds** that perform these **abominable ceremonies** have turned the words ANYONE, EVERYONE, AND WHOEVER DIVORCES and marries another commits adultery... into:
"NO ONE WHO DIVORCES AND MARRIES ANOTHER IS REALLY COMMITTING ADULTERY!!!"

Why do christians not TREMBLE at these verses?

Isaiah 66:2 NASB
"For My hand made all these things, Thus all these things came into being," declares the LORD

"But to *this one* I will look, To him who is humble and contrite of spirit, and who trembles at My word."

The following verse highlights the absolute refusal of many in the whore church to **"tremble"** when they lightly gloss over and attempt to diminish what Jesus plainly said in the 16th chapter of Luke's gospel. It is so easy to understand, but the carnal mind does not desire to acknowledge the truthfulness of Jesus' all encompassing statement regarding divorce and remarriage, nor does it desire to obey it.

Luke 16:18

NIV

"**Anyone** who divorces his wife and marries another woman commits adultery, and the man who marries a divorced woman commits adultery."

NLT

"For example, a man who divorces his wife and marries someone else commits adultery. And **anyone** who marries a woman divorced from her husband commits adultery."

KJV

"**Whosoever** putteth away his wife, and marrieth another, committeth adultery: and **whosoever** marrieth her that is put away from her husband committeth adultery."

YLT

"**Every one** who is sending away his wife, and marrying another, doth commit adultery; and **every one** who is marrying her sent away from a husband doth commit adultery."

ESV

"**Everyone** who divorces his wife and marries another commits adultery, and he who marries a woman divorced from her husband commits adultery."

Seems pretty straightforward does it not? There is no ambiguity whatsoever in any translation concerning this verse of scripture. But the liars will not accept this profound statement either.

Every Word of God is - True and Tested...? OR...

"can be easily circumvented by adding words like...
except for adultery, abandonment, prison, etc.?"

There is a very simple principle the Lord outlined to me as to why this passage is ignored and dismissed as authoritative in every instance and it isn't what most people would assume!

Here is one particular vow that my own whore of a wife made a covenant to keep - *"forsaking all other flesh, as long as you both shall live,"* and she said she would keep herself only for me...

BUT SHE IS CURRENTLY, WILLINGLY BEING FUCKED BY ANOTHER MAN AT THE WRITING OF THIS BOOK! AND NOT ONE OF THE HUNDREDS OF WITNESSES TO HER VOWS IS CALLING HER ON THE CARPET FOR HER TREACHERY AND ADULTERY!

Now, are you so dull witted to believe that Jesus plainly stated that we will all give account for even the smallest of careless idle words we speak, yet He will not hold those guilty who so treacherously betrayed practically EVERY WORD OF THEIR WEDDING VOWS???!!! The only thing that is unilateral, as far as the one making a covenant is concerned, is that no matter what the other person may do, you are still bound by those words. How many weddings have you been to where the bride and groom said:

"I DO, unless...

you commit adultery,

you abandon me,

you burn the pot roast,

you don't iron my socks...etc."

RIDICULOUS!

Now, let's move on to what is a covenant?

Chapter 2
What Makes A Covenant?

Malachi 2:14-16 NASB
"Yet you say, 'For what reason?' Because the LORD has been a witness between you and the wife of your youth, against whom you have dealt treacherously, though she is your companion and your wife by covenant *(BERIYTH)*. But not one has done so who has <u>a remnant of the Spirit</u>..**for I HATE divorce."**

Christians should get covenant more than anybody. The entire religion is supposedly based on the concept of someone **DYING... in order to bring about a NEW COVENANT!**

This is so seemingly simplistic, and yet I have not met very many christians who accept the validity of its meaning. A covenant is a solemn oath or vow that is always subject to the terms and conditions contained within it. There is a mountain of scripture (over 280 Hebrew REFERENCES for the word *BERIYTH* above, and over 30 Greek references for **DIATHEKE**) that confirm the tenet that it cannot be invalidated by anything other than the death of one of its parties. But, I am told over and over by goofballs, that **"adultery breaks the marital covenant."** I will address this issue in the next chapter.

Now, if you build on a crooked foundation, **BY IGNORING OVER 300 EXAMPLES IN SCRIPTURE, OF A COVENANT BEING LIFELONG,** then by the time you get to the upper stories you are far from being plumb. For now, I want to highlight some verses directly relating to the nature of what a covenant really is, and the kind of people that regularly make and break them.

Psalm 50:16 NASB
But to the wicked God says, "What right have you to tell of My statutes And to take **MY COVENANT** *(BERIYTH)* in your mouth?"

Proverbs 2:16 NASB
"To deliver you from the strange woman, From the adulteress who flatters with her words; That **leaves** the companion of her youth **And forgets the covenant *(BERIYTH)* of her God;** For her house sinks down to death And her tracks lead to the dead."

Now, here we have a definitive explanation of an integral aspect of what MUST OCCUR to invalidate any covenant, in order that a new one can be established:

Hebrews 9:15-17 NASB

For this reason He is the mediator of a **new covenant** *(DIATHEKE)*, so that, since a **death** has taken place for the redemption of the transgressions that were committed under the first covenant *(DIATHEKE)*, those who have been called may receive the promise of the eternal inheritance. For where a covenant *(DIATHEKE)* is, there must of necessity be the death of the one who made it. For a covenant *(DIATHEKE)* is valid only when men are dead, for it is never in force while the one who made it lives.

This is probably one of the most difficult passages in the Bible to understand, but the main point I want you to see is that a covenant binds the parties to its terms as long as they are both alive. I can't teach the deeper meaning of this passage because it is too high for the simple minded who reject Jesus' clear statements concerning **divorce and remarriage being adultery.**

Holy Whoredom

Look at this same passage in the literal for some clues and THEN FEEL FREE to make your own error riddled determination...

Hebrews 9:15-17 YLT

And because of this, of a new covenant he is mediator, that, death having come, for redemption of the transgressions under the first covenant, those called may receive the promise of the age-during inheritance, for where a covenant [is], **the death of the covenant-victim** to come in is necessary, for a **covenant over dead victims** [is] steadfast, since it is no force at all when the **covenant-victim** liveth...

Chew on that and maybe if you obey the marriage verses, the Lord will fill in the details on Hebrews 9 for you like He is filling them in for me! Now we need to go a little deeper into what really constitutes a covenant in God's determination:

Matthew 5:33-37 NLT

You have also heard that our ancestors were told, 'You must not break your vows; you must carry out the vows you make to the LORD.'
BUT I SAY, DO NOT MAKE ANY ANY ANY ANY VOWS! Do not say, 'By heaven!' because heaven is God's throne. And do not say, 'By the earth!' because the earth is his footstool. And do not say, 'By Jerusalem!' for Jerusalem is the city of the great King. Do not even say, 'By my head!' for you can't turn one hair white or black. **Just say a simple, 'Yes, I will,' or 'No, I won't.' Anything beyond this is from the evil one.**

NASB

Again, you have heard that the ancients were told,
YOU SHALL NOT MAKE FALSE VOWS, BUT SHALL FULFILL YOUR VOWS TO THE LORD.'
"BUT I SAY TO YOU, make no oath at all, either by heaven, for it is the throne of God, or by the earth, for it is the footstool of His feet, or by Jerusalem, for it is the city of the great king. "Nor shall you make an oath by your head, for you cannot make one hair white or black.

"But **let your statement be, 'Yes, yes' or 'No, no'; ANYTHING ... ANYTHING ... ANYTHING... BEYOND these is of evil.**"

Now what is Jesus saying here? I am going to give you a thoroughly original commentary on this verse. Jesus is telling us that when you make some pretense about your upcoming testimony, you are in effect saying:

"Hey, I am usually a deceitful liar that cannot be trusted, but since I am prefacing my words with a solemn oath, you can take my word for it!"

Jesus just raised the bar in the sermon on the mount as to what God demands from those wishing to enter God's Kingdom. He was saying all of our words are oaths, AND that we will give an account for every idle or careless word we ever speak. He also said this first, before His seven "BUT I SAY TO YOU" commands in Matthew 5, thereby abrogating the Mosaic laws He cited. People don't get that He was making the requirements of God even more, not less, strict.

Matthew 5:20 NASB

"For I say to YOU that UNLESS your righteousness *surpasses* that of the scribes and Pharisees, YOU...WILL NOT WILL NOT WILL NOT WILL NOT!...ENTER THE KINGDOM OF HEAVEN.

Grace doesn't **whitewash** YOUR **sin and rebellion** - grace **CAUSES YOU TO WALK IN OBEDIENCE**! YOUR **SINFUL WHORING** ONLY DEMONSTRATES THE LACK OF GOD'S GRACE IN YOUR LIFE.

Ezekiel 36:26-28 NASB

"Moreover, I will give you a **NEW HEART** and put a new spirit within you; and **I WILL REMOVE THE HEART OF STONE from your flesh and give you a heart of flesh.**

"I will put **My** Spirit within you and <u>**CAUSE**</u> <u>**CAUSE**</u> <u>**CAUSE**</u> <u>**CAUSE**</u>

YOU TO WALK in **My** statutes, (laws, rules, commands) *AND.....*

YOU WILL BE CAREFUL **TO OBSERVE MY ORDINANCES...**

I don't have time here to destroy the whole **"I was born again, but I still sin"** nonsense, but I will tell you that it is wholly blasphemous! **If you are in a remarriage, then YOU ARE <u>NOT</u> BORN AGAIN, AND NEITHER IS YOUR PASTOR!**

THE COVENANT WITH GIBEONITES

In Joshua 9, there is a story about a hastily entered into covenant by Joshua and the leaders of Israel not long after they came into the promised land. What you should do is read it for yourself. But here is the condensed version.

The people of Gibeon knew that their days were numbered because the armies of Israel were killing all of the inhabitants of Canaan in a devastating military campaign. Therefore, they hatched a scheme to save their bacon by using guile to trick Israel into making a covenant with them, so they would not be destroyed as a people.

Well, Israel's leadership didn't seek the Lord's counsel, so they foolishly made a binding pact not to kill them. Long story short, they had to let them survive as a people, even though they were one of the tribes that the Lord had directed to be exterminated, like all of the other pagan nations of the land. Even though the Gibeonites lied as to where they were from, the leadership could not kill them.

Now skip ahead about 500 years to 2 Samuel, Chapter 21. I want you to see just **HOW SERIOUSLY AND FOR HOW LONG** God recognizes and avenges covenant violations.

2 Samuel 21:1-9 NASB

Now there was a famine in the days of David for three years, year after year; and David sought the presence of the LORD. And the LORD said, **"It is for Saul and his bloody house, because he put the Gibeonites to death."**

So the king called the Gibeonites and spoke to them (now the Gibeonites were not of the sons of Israel but of the remnant of the Amorites, and the sons of Israel **made a covenant *(BERIYTH)* with them**, but Saul had sought to kill them in his zeal for the sons of Israel and Judah). Thus David said to the Gibeonites, "What should I do for you? And **HOW CAN I MAKE ATONEMENT** that you may bless the inheritance of the LORD?"

Then the Gibeonites said to him, "We have no concern of silver or gold with Saul or his house, nor is it for us to put any man to death in Israel." And he said, "I will do for you whatever you say." So they said to the king, "The man who consumed us and who planned to exterminate us from remaining within any border of Israel,

LET SEVEN MEN FROM HIS SONS BE GIVEN TO US, AND WE WILL HANG THEM BEFORE THE LORD

in Gibeah of Saul, the chosen of the LORD."

And the king said, "I will give them."....

Then he gave them into the hands of the Gibeonites, and they hanged them in the mountain before the LORD, so that the seven of them fell together; AND THEY WERE PUT TO DEATH in the first days of harvest at the beginning of barley harvest.

Even though the Gibeonites deceived Joshua initially...

God still viewed the terms of the covenant binding FOR GENERATIONS!

I know this is one issue that is always brought up, so here is as good a time as any to settle it. Some whore says:

"Well, I wasn't a christian when I got married the first time, SO! - that means God doesn't hold me accountable for my first marriage."

Too bad there isn't a font named *contention speak*! but Comic Sans will have to do. You probably think I just hate women don't you? This isn't about gender bias, and I will show you how I do not discriminate unfairly - God calls men whores and adulteresses too. It is about **AUTHORITY** which we will explore in a later chapter.

Stop being silly and stupid! God holds everyone accountable for their word, did you not read this chapter? You will always be bound to the first person you marry, as long as you both shall live...

WHETHER YOU WERE A CHRISTIAN OR NOT...

Galatians 3:15 NASB

Brethren, I speak in terms of **human relations**:

even though it is *only* **a man's covenant** *(DIATHEKE)*,

yet when it has been ratified, **no one sets it aside**

or adds conditions to it.

Why is this verse almost never applied to divorce? Even though it isn't directly referencing divorce per se, I can't see any reason why this should not be applied to the marital covenant.

When you said *til death* did you not mean *til death*? Or were those just meaningless words? God will hold you accountable for them because **HE WAS A WITNESS**! When you set it aside by divorce, you are in direct disobedience to the principle in Galatians 3. Paul is making a strong case that it is plain stupidity to set aside or add conditions to any covenant.

Why would you be so foolish to find another opportunity to NOT TREMBLE AT GOD'S WORD?

Many unqualified people pack churches to witness marriage covenants. If you are invited to be a witness, start taking the responsibility seriously, because God expects you to.

1 Corinthians 7:12-13

But to the rest I say, not the Lord, that if any brother has a wife who is an unbeliever, and she consents to live with him, **he must not divorce her.** And a woman who has an unbelieving husband, and he consents to live with her, **she must not send (divorce) her husband away**.

Let those words sink in. You have a clear command not to divorce an UNBELIEVER, **implying that the marriage was entered into before you became one,** *because* a true believer would not marry an unbeliever. That would not be compatible with an obedient heart that Ezekiel 36 describes. Faith and works are evidence of each other. So, God recognizes covenants regardless of the spiritual condition of the person.

There is no qualifier in any verse that makes a distinction between believers or nonbelievers, Jesus says... EVERYONE WHO DIVORCES...

EVERYONE, EVERYONE, EVERYONE, who divorces his wife and marries another commits adultery, and he who marries one who is divorced from a husband commits adultery.

So what did we learn about vows and covenants?

They are **unconditionally** binding until the one who made it DIES, this is altogether compatible with these two verses:

Romans 7:2-3 NASB

For the married woman **is bound by law to her husband WHILE he is LIVING**; but **if her husband DIES, she is released** from the law concerning the husband. So then,

IF *WHILE* her husband is LIVING

she is joined to another man,...

...she *shall* be called an adulteress

I am only doing as I am commanded to do, by calling women who fall under this circumstance, adulteresses and whores. I WILL ALSO CALL THE MEN WHO MARRY THEM WHOREMONGERS AND ADULTERERS. I AM NOTHING, IF I AM NOT AN EQUAL OPPORTUNITY INSULTER!

...but if her husband dies, she is free from the law, so that she is not an adulteress though she is joined to another man.

1 Corinthians 7:39 NASB

A wife is **bound as long as her husband lives**; but if her **husband is dead, she is free** to be married to whom she wishes, **only in the Lord.**

Why is this so hard to accept? Because the **carnal nature**, that **can only be rebellious and *enslaved* by its forbidden desires**, **cannot obey** this command to **remain faithful to its vows**.

If you really want to marry another, you may as well truly murder your mate. You are **guilty of it anyway**. Much less messy than divorce. You get everything, not just half! You can also have a clear conscience concerning adultery!

Of course, I am being facetious, but I ran into an idiot named James on his "christian" discussion forum, **that in all seriousness** made this ludicrous assertion.

Believer X

Mr. christian retard, James said:
I have been studying this subject for a bit now. As usual, I study Reformed preachers and theologians on this subject, and I look carefully at each Scripture verse that has been used on this subject. I will agree with bx that according to Scripture, God is either forbidding ALL RE-marriage WHILE the ex-spouse is alive, OR severely limiting it.

Now, IF God is forbidding ALL remarriage Then I would have to say without a doubt that there is SEVERE and systemic negligence on the part of preachers and pastors everywhere! You are telling me that Scripture forbids ALL remarriage while the ex-spouse is alive, and that I have been studying Scripture, reading great Christian works, listening to Christian radio, for twenty years, and I have not come across this until now???

The reality is that Christians and theologians are divided on this issue. I am still studying this, but there IS one thing I wish to put to rest and ANYONE who wishes to debate me on this, I am ready.

And that is the Idea that believerx put forth on this group, that THE ENTIRE TIME A CHRISTIAN IS RE-MARRIED THAT THEY ARE IN A CONTINUAL STATE OF ADULTERY. That idea is false. Now believerx didn't take it any further, but of Course others who read what believerx said immediately thought it through and went, "You mean that no matter what I do, I am in a continual state of adultery? That I should divorce my current spouse? What about the children?, etc etc."

Holding that false idea that bx put forth WILL lead ONLY to a catch-22 situation. You will say, Hey, I am married, but I was divorced, and my ex is still alive, so according to believerx, I am in a CONTINUAL STATE of adultery, so I should get divorced, EVEN though my spouse has only been married to me, and wait a minute, God HATES divorce!!!

So, you can see that this does not make sense, no matter HOW strict your belief is on re-marriage. I would ask anyone holding this position why God did not tell the men who already have multiple wives, to immediately divorce ALL of them but the FIRST one they married? According to bx's reasoning, the man and ALL the wives would be in a continual state of adultery!! Why is there no teaching on this? Why is there no command on this?

Now, forgetting that false concept for a moment, I would like to say that I personally don't like the idea of the innocent party in a divorce to have to suffer and be alone for the rest of their life because of what someone else did. And if you have been the innocent party of a divorce, and you strongly believe that re-marriage WHILE the ex is alive would have you living in a state of CONTINUAL sin, what is going to happen if you meet someone and have a strong desire to marry them?

<u>I think that could lead to murder!!!</u> Seriously, follow me on this: Okay, I married a person, loved them, was a good spouse, and they abandoned me, divorced me, and now I can't marry anyone WHILE they are alive, and I met someone and I SO want to marry them! I can either live in a CONTINUAL state of sin, because my ex is alive, OR......drum roll please...I can commit ONE sin, of murder, and then get married!!!"
Ta Da!

Needless to say, I was absolutely awestruck to see what I thought was merely an attribute - stupidity - become incarnate in the form of someone who claimed to be born again.

Believer X

Here is what I wrote in reply after I stopped howling with incredulous laughter:

JAMES,
I WILL REFRAIN FROM CALLING YOU AN IDIOT THIS TIME BECAUSE YOU SEEM TO BE OPEN TO THE TRUTH.
John 1:14 NASB
And the Word became flesh, and dwelt among us, and we saw His glory, glory as of the only begotten from the Father,
full of grace and truth.
full of grace and truth.
full of grace and truth.

John 1:17 NASB
For the Law was given through Moses;
(THIS SHOULD ANSWER YOUR POLYGAMY QUERY)
grace and truth
grace and truth
grace and truth
grace and truth were realized through Jesus Christ.

APPARENTLY YOU TAKE THIS TO MEAN:
FULL OF LICENTIOUSNESS (UNBRIDLED LUST) AND ENDLESS CONTRADICTIONS.

JAMES, THE THINGS YOU SAY ARE UTTER SILLINESS. IMAGINE, a person committed to living the torment of a celibate single life, WHILE THEIR COVENANT MATE IS HAVING SEXUAL INTERCOURSE WITH ANOTHER, in total obedience to Christ would then consider murder. This comes from your deluded mindset that only the act of marrying is adultery. It is an adulterous, murderous heart that is unclean from the inside the wayward mate possesses, not the victimized spouse.

IN ORDER TO MAKE YOUR CASE, YOU MUST THEN ACCEPT THAT STATEMENTS AND COMMANDS OF CHRIST IN SCRIPTURE ARE SOMEHOW NULLIFIED BY OTHERS.

1 Corinthians 7 NASB
10But to the married I give instructions, not I, but the Lord, that the wife should not leave her husband
(UNCONDITIONALLY TRUE OR CONDITIONALLY TRUE???)

11(but if she does leave, she must remain unmarried,
(UNCONDITIONALLY TRUE OR CONDITIONALLY TRUE???)

or else be reconciled to her husband),
(UNCONDITIONALLY TRUE OR CONDITIONALLY TRUE???)

and that the husband should not divorce his wife.
(UNCONDITIONALLY TRUE OR CONDITIONALLY TRUE???)

12But to the rest I say, not the Lord, that if any brother has a wife who is an unbeliever, and she consents to live with him, he must not divorce her.
(UNCONDITIONALLY TRUE OR CONDITIONALLY TRUE???)

13And a woman who has an unbelieving husband, and he consents to live with her, she must not send her husband away.
(UNCONDITIONALLY TRUE OR CONDITIONALLY TRUE???)

39A wife is bound as long as her husband lives;
(UNCONDITIONALLY TRUE OR CONDITIONALLY TRUE???)

but if her husband is dead, she is free to be married to whom she wishes, only in the Lord.

Matthew 19 NASB
6"So they are no longer two, but one flesh.
(UNCONDITIONALLY TRUE OR CONDITIONALLY TRUE???)

What therefore God has joined together, let no man separate."
Just because man separates them, does not mean or even imply that GOD DOES - ONLY DEATH CAN NULLIFY A COVENANT - WHICH IS WHAT MARRIAGE IS.

OK JAMES, what about all those supposed ONE-TIME SINFUL CEREMONIES? DOES THAT MEAN GOD PARTICIPATED IN THE COVENANT - AND NOW HE CAN SOMEHOW VALIDATE IT, HOW DOES THAT WORK? JUST CURIOUS. PLEASE PROVIDE VOLUMINOUS SCRIPTURAL REFERENCES.

HOW DOES HE MAKE TWO ONE, IF THE ACT ITSELF IS ADULTERY? AND WHO WOULD PERFORM THEM? MINISTERS OF THE GOSPEL? THINK JAMES, THINK.

Believer X

KEEP STUDYING AND KEEP ACCUMULATING TEACHERS TO YOURSELF...I AM "TRYING" TO BE AS POLITE AS I CAN. Believerx

THEN I replied with this a couple of days later, after more nonsense on James' part:
Do you think your murder scenario in order to release someone from their vows was very intellectually valid? I thought it was pure delusional nonsense. That someone who would be committed to suffering the behavior of their mate, would even consider killing them and covering it up to marry another person. Having the counsel of the LORD doesn't make me smarter, it only makes me right. - BX

He never did anything, but avoid the central issue because he already admitted he would only listen to the consensus of those "scholars" in the majority of mainstream christianity, which I was in opposition to.

Did you happen to notice that he failed to quote a single verse of scripture in his argument where he made the confident assertion that **my entire premise was false**?

There are examples in scripture where God still honors a covenant even though one party has abandoned the other, where one party is even deceived on the wedding day, and where one party has committed grievous sexual sin.

Let's look at 5 practical examples of unbroken covenant marriages God gives us.

Jacob and Leah

(Genesis 29:21-26)
Here is the short version. Jacob fled to Haran and fell in love with Rachel - the pretty one. He wasn't all that into Leah because she was a dog, but she was older. Laban, Leah's father, tricked Jacob into marrying Leah, when Jacob thought he was actually marrying Rachel.

So, even a marriage covenant that is entered into by ignorance and deception, was still binding. Jacob had sex with Leah after he got drunk at the reception, so he couldn't obtain a divorce.

David and Michal

(1 Samuel 18:20-28, 1 Samuel 25:44, 2 Samuel 3:13-16)
Saul gave his daughter Michal to David for the dowry David paid him. They were married, but as is often the case trouble brewed and festered between in-laws. Saul wanted David dead - David split town, Saul annulled Michal and David's marriage and gave her to Palti.

Skip ahead...
Saul is dead and David is king over Judah. Abner is his chief opponent and is all that is left of team Saul. Abner is getting his butt kicked in every way imaginable by David. He wants to make a covenant of peace and abdicate to David's authority. David says, **"Oh yeah?! well here is what I demand.** Michal is my wife, go get her and bring her to me or you're **FINISHED."** So Abner gets Michal from her husband Palti and returns her to David, her rightful husband.

For those who use Deut. 24:1 (by misapplying it) to justify staying in a remarriage and not reconciling with the first spouse, in this case, David would have been guilty of an abomination. Not so, the only covenant that is valid until death is the first one, this highlights the **scriptural principle of leaving an adulterous union and returning to your covenant spouse.**

Herod and Herodias

John the Baptist comes on the scene – tells Herod that he is in an unlawful marriage with his brother Phillip's wife, Herodias. This enrages Herodias no doubt, because John would have quoted the scriptures in Proverbs concerning adulteresses and whores. The only way to get John to shut up, was for Herodias to figure out a way to get John's head removed from his body. That is the nature of Jezebel, to teach error and lead you astray in this area of marriage and divorce, as well as to persecute the John the Baptists whom God always sends to the rebellious house of Israel.

Hosea and Gomer

This is probably the most outrageous example found in the Bible of a marital covenant NOT BEING broken by the most grievous sin and sexual uncleanness.

In Hosea 1, the Lord tells Hosea to go and marry a whore, the very first time He speaks to him. No small talk or chit chat, the first words from God to Hosea were, **"Go and marry a whore"** (Jerusalem Bible translation). This is what also happened to me the night of March 11, 1986. God told me to marry a whore (even though I thought she was a christian and desired to be godly), Mary Mileur, who was my girlfriend at the time. Well, we both (Hosea and I) obeyed and found ourselves bound to contentious, stubborn, unsubmissive wives.

Gomer became a temple prostitute to worship and serve Baal. She no doubt had intercourse with hundreds, if not thousands of men. Then what happened? God told Hosea to go marry Gomer again in chapter 3, after wickedness had overtaken her, and she rebelled against the husband of her youth. That is why I believe my wife will either repent of her whoring one day, or God will kill her prematurely, like He smote Tammy Faye Bakker/Messner with cancer for her treachery against her husband Jim Bakker. God is never mocked for very long. Recompense for covenant breaking will come quickly.

Keep Hosea in mind as we go into the next chapter addressing the "exception" to divorce for adultery. Hmmm...

Malachi 2

In case you missed the first verse I quoted in this chapter, then read it again. This verse proves that divorce doesn't dissolve a marriage - she is still his WIFE by covenant AFTER he treacherously divorces her (he is an "unbeliever who leaves" as well). But she is still bound to him! It is mind-boggling how people completely ignore this passage or explain it away. If God says that He **HATES DIVORCE**, why would we even flirt with something that God hates, much less actually do it?

This chapter on covenants was about 10 times shorter than I could have made it! Don't you think with over 300 examples to draw from, that I could have absolutely demolished your silly notion about the fairy tale of adultery nullification? I let you off EASY! Now let's look at adultery, and how it is irrelevant as it pertains to the marriage bond being inviolate as long as both parties are alive.

Chapter 3
Adultery/Fornication
The Exception – OH...*really*?
Innocent Party?
C'mon...give me a break!

Now, let's break down the **"exception clause"** and **"innocent party teachings"** with all of the lies and misinformation surrounding them. Read Matthew 5:31-32 and 19:3-12.

Wow, there sure isn't a lot here, only two verses that deal with the exception directly. But **where *exactly* does it say:**

"You can divorce for adultery and then remarry, since I would never want you to be deprived of love, affection, and sexual intimacy?"

Because that is the resultant assumption of these **damnable heresies.** PLEASE POINT IT OUT TO ME.

Matthew 5:31-32 NASB

It was said, 'WHOEVER SENDS HIS WIFE AWAY, LET HIM GIVE HER A CERTIFICATE OF DIVORCE'...

Believer X

THIS IS WHAT YOU ARE PINNING ALL YOUR HOPES ON. PAY ATTENTION TO EVERY **TESTED WORD!**

But I say to you...
But I say to you...
But I say to you...

THIS IS JESUS SPEAKING DIRECTLY TO YOU!!!

..that EVERYONE who divorces his wife...

Everyone? *Really* Jesus? *EVERYONE?*

Now here comes your precious little gnat (just three little Greek words) that you have so carefully strained from God's Word to build into a convoluted abomination of denial to virtually every other text in the Greek scriptures!

...except for the reason of unchastity...

porneia - *(fornication, unchastity, marital unfaithfulness)*

Let's set aside the precise meaning of that word **porneia** and look at other aspects of this passage in the light of other texts. Now what it does <u>**NOT**</u> say, is **just as important** as what it in fact does say. **It does NOT say:**

"You may divorce your wife for adultery, and then marry another without committing adultery"

...makes her commit ...

(or causes her to commit *fornication?* NO!)

...ADULTERY...

(Gr. moicheia *definition: unlawful sexual relations with the spouse of another. When used in a literal application it is a sexual ACT at its core.)* This is a different Greek word entirely than the one above for **unchastity.** You have Jesus making a distinction in the very same sentence between two differing sexual acts:

Holy Whoredom

Fornication - premarital sex (in this case during betrothal), before a marriage covenant is made

Adultery - extramarital sex during the marriage, after you are bound for life by the words of your oath!

But you want them to be equivalent, in the very context where He sets them apart from each other! That is only being swayed by your preconceived bias of wanting to validate your whoring. I will play along and humor your blatant disregard of the distinction Jesus Himself makes and concede **it *could* mean adultery too.**

SO...now let's look at the passage from a different angle, keeping in mind that I will **consistently** apply <u>your</u> definition of adultery to the Greek word that is almost universally translated as something different than adultery. Are you really sure you want to do this? Because this may hurt after you pull yourself up from off of the canvas!

The innocent party doctrine states in a mind bending number of variations that some divorced people may remarry under a certain set of prescribed convoluted circumstances. I don't have time to list all 31 flavors here.

Let's take a practical example of what this type of teaching is saying in a real life situation. Joe and Judy get married, and it is a first marriage for both (covenant). Joe doesn't like the way she cooks spaghetti, so he drags her before the unrighteous courts and obtains a one-sided no fault divorce, despite her being willing to do anything to make the marriage work. "No way! Jennifer will treat me right," he says. He is implacable and he marries Jennifer.

They shuttle the children back and forth as dictated by the godless family court system. Judy is under constant financial strain. She is weary and without hope. She wants her family to be restored, but she joins a great new church and meets a *"Bible believing"* christian man, Tom, to whom her pimp, er... I mean pastor, introduces her. She keeps herself sexually pure until they get married. They consummate their love, and it is wonderful and satisfying. **How could this not be God's will?**

Yet, Jesus says, SHE IS COMMITTING ADULTERY.

Matthew 5:32 NASB
<u>Everyone</u> who divorces his wife, except for the reason of unchastity, <u>makes her commit adultery</u>; and whoever marries a divorced woman commits adultery.

Even though she did nothing wrong to merit a divorce, according to your totally fabricated exception nonsense, she is still guilty of sexual sin, which her first husband will be accountable for, and her new husband will be judged for. If you want to play with this verse and mishandle it, it will burn you every time. You cannot deny or refute what I just said. You have an explicit statement condemning the most verifiably innocent party (Judy), as an adulteress.

"Everyone who divorces his wife, except for the reason of unchastity,
MAKES HER COMMIT ADULTERY."

But you want to stubbornly insist that God will judge Judy for adultery if she remarries, but no one else of the millions of American christians who are divorced and remarried? You are so illogical and ignorant of the words in the text that you pulled out of the BROAD SCRIPTURES - the rest came out of your ass!

THY COMMANDMENT IS EXCEEDINGLY BROAD!!!

But you want to make it hang on those 3 *exceedingly* narrow words: **"except for unchastity"**...and change every rule of grammar, context, meaning, logic, and sound reasoning, solely based on you desperately wanting something THAT deep in your heart you know is unlawful - even though you won't admit it.

BECAUSE:

Proverbs 30:20 NKJV

THIS is the way of an adulterous woman;
she eats, and wipes her mouth, and says,
I have done NO wickedness!!!

Yes, you have...
A LOT of WICKEDNESS.

It is amazing how many divorced christian women, when confronted with the truth of the scriptures concerning this sound doctrine, will lose that "***sweet precious spirit***" and turn into someone filled with hate and vitriol. You think I use inappropriate language? Here is an email I received from Cathy, an adulteress, "who loves the Lord." I guess this is how she interprets **"Love your enemies!"** Cathy wrote:

You never taught me anything. You never told me what to do, except 'repent', whatever the hell that meant. You just yelled at me & called me names, while withholding your 'truth'.

Fuck off & die, believerx . See you in HELL.

&, BTW, I didn't tell you WHY we're not having sex. It's because we can't, so FUCK YOU & THAT HOLE IN YOUR FACE!!!!!!

Cathy

She spends her time online posting worthless christian articles and discussing her great revelations. Yet, when I reproved her for adamantly refusing to stop committing her unclean sexual activity with irrefutable teaching, she became as violent as Herodias wanting my head! More on that later. Look what happens when Joe's bitterness and unforgiveness runs its course and ends in divorce:

Hebrews 12:14-15 NASB

Pursue peace with all men, and the **sanctification** without which no one will see the Lord. See to it that no one comes short of the grace of God; that **no root of bitterness** springing up **causes trouble**, and by it <u>**MANY** be defiled</u>...

Believer X

Back to Judy...if she was divorced for anything other than adultery (according to your own misinterpretation), and she is compelled to remarry out of self preservation or loneliness, then she is defiled, her children are defiled, and her new husband is defiled. If he has been divorced and has children, they are are defiled, Joe is defiled, Jenny is defiled. If Jenny has children, they are defiled. Like ripples in a pond from the toss of a single stone, it infects everyone associated with uncleanness, and the Lord will lay a large chunk of the blame at the door of her covenant husband JOE!

So, according to your reasoning, if you really believe the verse teaches divorce and remarriage is permitted as long as the woman committed adultery, then you must accept the same premise that if she is not guilty of adultery and she subsequently remarries, then she will be committing adultery in the next marriage. You must acknowledge this. You have no statements from any other text to make a legitimate argument.

So, by her sinning (committing adultery), her next marriage can be valid - because the adultery, I am told, breaks the covenant (in some, not all circles), *but* if she is without guilt, then her next marriage **must be considered sinful** (adulterous). This is the lunacy of the innocent party heresy - more like **"Hey, let's punish the innocent and reward the wicked"**. That is what you are essentially doing, because you cannot find anything in the text that Jesus said to nullify the adultery of the innocent woman who remarries! Do you see anything wrong with that logic?

You are accusing Jesus of something outrageously and wildly inequitable with your blasphemous exception assertion. I used the very passage you use to justify divorce and remarriage in cases of adultery, but Jesus says the innocent of adultery will be sinning in the event they remarry.

Fall to your knees and beg the Lord's mercy for such evil accusations against HIM!

...and **WHOEVER** marries a divorced woman commits adultery.

I think I effectively covered this above, but just in case you missed it, there is that TESTED word WHOEVER! But what is notable in this phrase, is what it implies - that he is having sexual RELATIONS with the wife of ANOTHER man. This can only be **referring to husband NUMERO UNO, GENIUS!**

But the reality is, nobody actually enforces ANY standards at all. Everything is just under the blanket of God's imaginary forgiveness.

Second *exception* text:

Matthew 19:3 NASB

Some Pharisees came to Jesus, testing Him and asking, **"Is it lawful** for a man to divorce his wife **for any reason at all?"**

Here is the **circumcision party** of His day, testing God because they want **"any reason."** That is the essence of this book - how lying clergymen and Jezebels change Jesus' strict policy from EVERYONE is committing adultery to **"NO ONE is committing adultery!"**

Even the Pharisees would not have been so stupid as the modern day **circumcision** is - **today's demonic preachers** allow women to divorce their husbands without even a hint from scripture that it is allowed! That is how far they have abandoned the Word of God! This is the real meaning of **subversion (upsetting families) in Titus 1** - **overthrowing** God's ordained order of **family authority**. Giving women rebellious **hardened hearts** against their husbands, to whom they are **commanded to be in submissive obedience.**

Matthew 19:4-6 NASB
And He answered and said, "**Have you not read** that He who created them from the beginning MADE THEM MALE AND FEMALE, and said, 'FOR THIS REASON A MAN SHALL LEAVE HIS FATHER AND MOTHER AND BE JOINED TO HIS WIFE, AND THE TWO SHALL BECOME ONE FLESH'? "So they are no longer two, **but one flesh.** What therefore God has joined together, let no man separate."

ONE FLESH?

BUT SOMEHOW AN EARTHLY DIVORCE CAN UNDO A MYSTICAL UNION CREATED BY GOD. **WE'LL SEE.**

LET NOT MAN SEPARATE?

This is not some idle suggestion. This is a command, that if broken, there will be severe penalties for anybody who destroys or **subverts a family**! This means lawyers, judges, preachers, friends, and family members (in-laws, brothers, sisters, children). **God will severely punish** everyone who advocated or abetted divorce!

Matthew 19:7-12 NASB
They said to Him, "Why then did Moses command to GIVE HER A CERTIFICATE OF DIVORCE AND SEND her AWAY?" He said to them, "**Because of your hardness of heart** Moses permitted you to divorce your wives; **but from the beginning it has not been this way.** "And I say to you, **whoever divorces his wife...**

Whoever is used again...here is your second gnat to strain

...except for immorality (Matthew 5:32 says "unchastity")...

Why is the English word different in this passage? Same exact Greek word in Matthew 5 above - could it be to keep **you poor stupid sheep confused?** It is **"porneia"** - fornication (premarital sex).

...and marries another woman commits adultery...

...The disciples said to Him, "If the relationship of the man with his wife is like this, it is better not to marry." But He said to them, "**Not all men can accept** this statement, but only those to whom it has been given. "For there are eunuchs who were born that way from their mother's womb; and there are eunuchs who were made eunuchs by men; and there are also eunuchs who made themselves eunuchs for the **sake of the Kingdom of Heaven...**

...He who is able to accept this, let him accept it.

Now the disciples seemed to understand what Jesus was saying: That if you marry, no matter what happens, **you will be locked into your commitments**. Then, Jesus told them something extra. He said that if it comes down to it, **you** might not be able to have sex anymore, because of a living wife or husband who has divorced you. But, He prefaced it by saying **you** would not accept the hard standards that **you** would possibly have to live by in order to enter the Kingdom of Heaven. That **you** could be forced into a celibate life that is beyond your control. Not fair, but it is a standard of righteousness that the Lord requires, and it was in the context of His teaching on divorce. So, are **you** sure that remarriage is an option in the light of this pronouncement?

Are **you** willing to roll the dice and gamble away your spot in God's Kingdom based only on theory and conjecture that He authorized remarriage as the result of a legitimate divorce? **You** have no statement that actually says you can remarry. It is an argument only from silence and assumption.

It does say, **you can divorce for porneia,** whatever that means. The Jews had the most liberal meaning for porneia - they could divorce, **only a wife,** for any reason, including her burning the goat burgers, and the Jews/christians still do the same thing today! Only now they allow a woman to usurp the authority of her husband by taking him to court and putting him away unlawfully.

I will not even argue the meaning here *of porneia* - it has been beaten to death without any resolution - it is pointless...

My sword will find a better spot to strike the fatal blow to your carnal mentality!

But, it doesn't explicitly say you may **remarry** another. You are adding words that do not appear in the text. **HE TOLD YOU, do not add to His Word - YOU LIAR!**

Look at what it does **not** say:

"If you happen to divorce your wife for adultery, you may marry another without any fear of committing adultery."

Nope! Not there! And again only a man may divorce for cause. Nowhere in scripture does Jesus give a woman the right to divorce her husband FOR ANY REASON!

Here is the short version. Contained within those three words, you have the exception, as it really is to be applied from the only actual practical example found in scripture:

You are a Jewish man in 1st century Israel, who meets a nice girl (or so you think!). She comes from a respectable family, so you ask for her hand in marriage. You make certain promises contingent upon her sexual purity being confirmed on the wedding night. You have a one year period of betrothal, when you make preparations to receive your bride unto yourself. A couple of months after these initial commitments were made, you are horrified to learn that your "good" little Jewish princess is pregnant with what cannot possibly be your child. Still caring for her reputation and not wanting to raise another man's kid (since they can't be of your lineage), you decide to put her away (divorce her) privately.

No courts, no paperwork, no covenant to break, no heart-breaking custody arrangements for your children. She is merely betrothed to you. You have not acted treacherously, because you made your pledge **based on her remaining pure** until your wedding day, but it appears she has **played the harlot** with another man and is lacking in restraint. **Sound familiar?**

Matthew 1:18-19 NLT

This is how Jesus the Messiah was born. His mother, Mary, was **engaged** to be married to Joseph. But **before the marriage took place,** while she was still a virgin, she became pregnant through the power of the Holy Spirit. Joseph, her fiancé, was a good man and did not want to **disgrace her publicly,** so he decided to break the engagement **(Greek** *to divorce her)* quietly.

Holy Whoredom

CEV

Joseph was a good man and did not want to embarrass Mary in front of everyone. So he decided to quietly call off the wedding.

That is a good contemporary understanding, but here are the literal words in the Greek text that **I WANT YOU TO PAY CLOSE ATTENTION TO:**

YLT

And of Jesus Christ, the birth was thus: For his mother Mary having been **betrothed** to Joseph, **before their coming together** she was found to have conceived from the Holy Spirit, and Joseph **her husband** being righteous, and not willing to make her an example, did wish privately to send her away (DIVORCE HER).

Here are the next pertinent texts that are to be carefully scrutinized in comparison to the Matthew 5 and 19 "exception passages."

Mark 10:11 NASB

And He said to them, **"Whoever divorces his wife and marries another woman commits adultery against her..."**

I am looking for your all encompassing exception clause...*where oh where can it be?* Is it hiding in Mark somewhere else? because Mark was writing to Roman believers who did not have access to Matthew's gospel. I wonder why the Holy Spirit was so forgetful in informing Roman christians of their Divine right to throw away their unwanted spouses for something as offensive as adultery? Wow! Don't be so dull witted, there is no exception for marital divorce whatsoever, only betrothal divorce. That is why it is only found in Matthew's gospel, which was written to Jews (who practiced betrothal) - Romans did not, and neither do Americans.

...and if she herself divorces her husband and marries another man, she is committing adultery."

Here you have the one passage that covers a woman obtaining a divorce. Again, no exception is available for women. How sexist of Jesus - what a pig!

Luke 16:18 NASB

EVERYONE who divorces his wife and marries another commits adultery, and he who marries one who is divorced from a husband commits adultery.

The Gospel of Luke was written to Greeks, another culture that did not require Luke to include your fanciful exception. They didn't practice betrothal either, and both Greek and Roman cultures allowed women to divorce, whereas Jewish culture did not. (More on the gender specific differences in a later chapter.)

So, according to your exception clause, what you have is a sexist, racist (Jesus) who allowed only Jewish men to divorce for adultery, but He denied the same right to Romans and Greeks (Gentiles) and women. This is how insane the exception heresy is, when really put to the test of the rest of scripture. It is entirely motivated by selfishness and carnality - fleshly driven desires.

Here is what Paul had to say to the Corinthians (Greeks) in what is the most comprehensive passage in scripture on the subject of marriage and divorce:

1 Corinthians 7:10-11 NASB

But to the married I give instructions, **not I, but the Lord, that the wife should not leave her husband...**

**Hard to understand?
Not for anyone with a brain!**

...(but if she does leave, **she must remain unmarried, or else be reconciled** to her husband)...

You have a contingency for a woman in a potentially dangerous situation. This is only a concession to protect herself from possibly a volatile husband. Remember, this is written to a believing woman.

She is under her husband's authority, she may only leave - not divorce, not remarry, not seek any monetary support through the unrighteous courts - to get out of a physically abusive situation (which would not even be an issue if she obeyed the command to be **quiet and respectful.** Men do not beat **submissive women.** They only **beat mouthy, contentious ones**). It is her job to **save her unbelieving husband.**

The wife is bound, so any remarriage **cannot be sanctified.** Therefore Paul, fully aware of the exception (having been a Jewish Rabbi), did not include it in this lengthy letter. Why not?

Jesus **taught Paul the Gospel by revelation.** How could Paul be so derelict as to not include what is such an important aspect of divorce - a legitimate reason? He already informed you in chapter 6 that **you cannot go to court for any reason whatsoever.** Tell me how you can obtain a divorce without breaking this unconditional prohibition condemning it? **And if you do, then you are...** forfeiting your inheritance in God's Kingdom along with sodomites, fornicators, idolaters, adulterers, effeminate, thieves, the covetous, drunkards, revilers, and swindlers.

1 Corinthians 7:11b-12 NASB

...and that the husband **should not divorce his wife**.

Again, no exception mentioned. Just a flat commandment, **NO DIVORCE.**

...But to the rest I say, not the Lord, that if any brother has a wife who is an unbeliever, and she consents to live with him, **he must NOT divorce her**.

Now, if she is an unbeliever, then what is she likely to do? What is the scripturally accurate depiction of an unbeliever's behavior?

Galatians 5:19-21 NASB

Now the **deeds of the flesh are evident,** which are: **immorality** (PORNEIA - fornication), impurity, sensuality, idolatry, sorcery, enmities, strife, jealousy, outbursts of anger, disputes, dissensions, factions, envying, drunkenness, carousing, and things like these, of which I forewarn you, just as I have forewarned you, that those who practice such things will not inherit the kingdom of God.

Paul knew what he was requiring of a **believing husband - to love his wife** and **endure** anything she may do. Does Love quit or does it **hope, believe, and endure all things**? **Can love fail?**

1 Corinthians 7:13 NASB
...And a woman who has an unbelieving husband, and he consents to live with her, <u>she must not send her husband away</u>...

Same thing goes for a woman - **she must love and endure** mistreatment. That is the way **into the Kingdom - by suffering!**

Acts 14:22 NASB
Through many tribulations we must enter the kingdom of God.

1 Corinthians 7:14-16 NASB
...For the unbelieving husband is sanctified through his wife, and the unbelieving wife is sanctified through her believing husband; for otherwise your children are unclean, but now they are holy...

Sanctification of the wayward spouse is the duty of the believing spouse - not to turn tail and run! You are also protecting your children's ultimate sanctification.

...Yet if the unbelieving one leaves, let him leave; the brother or the sister is not under **bondage** in such cases, but God has called us to peace.
Here is that other little pesky misinterpreted gnat, **"bondage"**. A close look at the Greek word in this verse, and the one in verse 39 **"bound"**, reveals that they have absolutely zero similarity to one another in the Greek. But conveniently, the translators can add confusion to promote the false doctrine that this is releasing you from the covenant. It ONLY means you are not under any obligation to serve someone who deserts you, but you are required to remain unmarried and...

...For how do you know, O wife,
whether you will save your husband?
Or how do you know, O husband,
whether you will save your wife?

Holy Whoredom

Now he just said that you were not under bondage, but then in the same breath he says that you can save the spouse who just deserted you. You can't pick and choose what you want to apply. It is all authoritative.

The writers of the Greek scriptures all knew each other and were inspired by the same Holy Spirit. Why is there such a conspicuous absence of your all important exception clause in any letter or gospel narrative written to Gentiles? Ask that question to your abominable pastor! Watch him squirm and try to B.S. his way out of that one!

Chapter 4
Genuine Righteousness

Isaiah 1:26
"Then I will restore your judges as at the first, And your counselors as at the beginning; <u>After that</u> you will be called the city of righteousness, A faithful city."

You might be asking...

"Why would a book about divorce and adultery contain a chapter on righteousness?"

If you are in deception about anything that is manifesting something as lawless and vile as remarital adultery, while claiming to follow Christ, then it has deep roots that are causing it.

You do not know that remarriage is adultery because you have only been taught error all of your christian experience. **Correction and training in righteousness** starts with truth and what it is, and what it means to be righteous before the Lord. I don't speak idle empty words. I can only produce good fruit, so hear what I say concerning **the real root cause of your dilemma...**

Holy Whoredom

Matthew 3:10 NASB

The ax is already laid at the **root of the trees;** therefore **EVERY EVERY EVERY EVERY** tree that does not bear good fruit is cut down and

thrown into the fire.

Ephesians 6:14 NASB

Stand firm therefore, **HAVING _GIRDED_ YOUR _LOINS_ WITH TRUTH, and HAVING PUT ON THE BREASTPLATE OF RIGHTEOUSNESS,**

NIV - with the belt of truth **buckled** around your **waist**

I started with truth - as the belt to gird your naked loins - genitals that commit acts of fornication both literal (whoring with another person's spouse) and spiritual - worshiping a foreign demon god under the guise of Jehovah. Don't bother denying the latter, just in case you happen to be guiltless of the former. It only means the outside of your cup is clean in this area.

Jesus told the churches that they were guilty of tolerating Jezebel and she teaches you in the ways of her Sidonian sex goddess Ashtoreth, and in Acts 19 Paul had a tangle with the church at Ephesus, with those who followed Artemis. She is the same vile demon goddess, just another variation - **NOTHING NEW**. By the time we get to Revelation 17 she is called:

"BABYLON THE GREAT, THE MOTHER OF HARLOTS AND OF THE ABOMINATIONS OF THE EARTH."

She is the woman drunk with the blood of the saints, and with the blood of the witnesses of Jesus.

It is interesting to note here in Ephesians 6, that NIV uses the words "buckled" and "waist". Whereas NASB uses the literal words "girded" and "loins". Why?

Believer X

I found many instances where all translations conceal the meaning, hindering understanding, so that you can never make progress in the truth. God's words are primarily spiritual in nature. Maybe I will write a book on that someday, but you must understand the relevance of first things first - I need you to repent (think clearly by changing your mind), before I will be able to unlock God's mysteries for you.

It has taken me years to acquire God's armor and His weapons of warfare. Not by some meaningless prayer ritual where you repeat Ephesians 6 into empty air, but the actual **engrafting of God's word** changing the way I think and behave. BUT YOU MUST START WITH **YOUR LOINS GIRDED WITH TRUTH**, which is <u>always</u> accompanied by grace. **GRACE AND TRUTH CAME BY JESUS CHRIST.**

Scarcely covering your **shameful sexual sins** with the fig leaf that your pastor **(the devil)** provided, is unable to conceal your **shame and harlotry** from someone who actually walks with the Lord. I see right through you. ALL YOU HAVE TO DO IS SPEAK OR WRITE SOMETHING ABOUT YOUR DOCTRINE, AND THE BLASPHEMIES THAT PROCEED FROM YOUR MOUTH ARE AS EVIDENT TO ME AS IF YOU WERE ACTUALLY VOMITTING AT MY FEET! I am a **spiritual** man - not bragging, just stating a fact. Your pastor is a ***carnal clown***, and therefore, **not approved of God.**

So, if you have received the truth and are really ashamed, I can begin to cloak you in God's righteousness. I am your servant bringing legitimate salvation to you, building into you things that make for righteousness. Do you want to be like the crowd or do you **HUNGER AND THIRST FOR RIGHTEOUSNESS**?

It is God who brings the famine to your soul, and it is He who fills you. But He uses a handful of men in every generation... not many - few. These are all basic biblical principles that are largely ignored. God says **countless teachers, but not many fathers. We are not like the many that peddle or corrupt God's Word.**

Even in writing this and attempting to go through traditional publishing, I don't know how He will guide my path, but I am not doing this for money. I don't have any now and that is not any real motivation for me. It used to be, when I was under the influence of the false gospel. The false gospel is the old wine that Jesus was referring to. **Everyone likes the old and hates the new.** The old isn't literal Judaism. Christians and Jews don't have any real disharmony anymore. They are all Gentiles from a heavenly perspective - **alienated from God's life (Eph. 4:17-19).**

So, what does real righteousness look like?

Well, the short answer is it looks like Jesus. Not the warm fuzzy Jesus that accepts you **"just as I am, without one plea..."** No, the real Jesus. He may take you initially like that, but He has to do some radically harsh things in order to transform you. I can't possibly distill my vast understanding of true righteousness into a few chosen phrases. I can, however, quote some verses that will give you a clue.

None of these chapters are even close to being comprehensive in their scope. I am merely hitting the bullet points. One book will not cover all of these topics in any great depth. The deep things of God are exceedingly deep. You are not ready for them yet - you are a baby. From here, you will have to open the scriptures, read, meditate, and **most importantly DO!**

<u>YOUR problem:</u>
Much BIGGER than you think!

Since righteousness is the admitted solution to "NOT being in right standing with God", then it would be helpful to categorize how God views people. You are either righteous or unrighteous. There is no sliding scale - **you are either totally WICKED or totally GOOD.**

Now without going into some deeper principles that do not violate what I just said, you are 2 people, one is **dead IN TRESSPASSES AND SINS**, and the other is yet to be created. Depending on your progress in the gospel, which is more complex than you can imagine, you have a problem. **You are under the yoke of slavery to sin.**

Believer X

Now, most people do not want to acknowledge the depth of their sinfulness. You compare yourself to the most wicked person you can think of, and are convinced that you are not as bad as the most notorious criminals, like serial killers and pedophiles. I want you to separate acts and behavior from what lies within you. I don't discount the value of making decisions regarding how we relate to people based on their actions.

But Jesus said:

Luke 13:1-5 NASB

Now on the same occasion there were some present who reported to Him about the Galileans whose blood Pilate had mixed with their sacrifices. And Jesus said to them, "**Do you suppose that** these Galileans **were greater sinners** than **all** other Galileans because they suffered this fate?"...

(I just love all those preachers who were so cocksure that hurricane Katrina or the earthquake in Haiti was God's wrath poured out upon the wicked. Well, this is one statement that would seem to contradict that kind of mentality.)

..."**I tell you, no,** but unless you repent, you will **all likewise perish.**

"Or **do you suppose** that those eighteen on whom the tower in Siloam fell and killed them were **worse culprits than all the men who live in Jerusalem?** "I tell you, no, but unless you repent, **you will all likewise perish."**

The implication Jesus is clearly making is everybody is equally bad. There are only 2 types of trees good and bad. Now, it would take 3 books to run down all of the scripture just covering good and bad trees in the Bible.

So the inference can be made that everyone is a bad or evil tree initially. I want to call your attention to Matthew 7 - please read the whole chapter.

Holy Whoredom

Matthew 7:1, 9-11, 15-20, 23 NASB

"**Do not judge so that you will not be judged.** "Or what man is there among you who, when his son asks for a loaf, will give him a stone? "Or if he asks for a fish, he will not give him a snake, will he?

"If you then, being evil, being evil, being evil..."

(Jesus made a blanket statement painting everyone with the same brush - EVIL!)

...know how to give good gifts to your children, how much more will your Father who is in heaven give what is good to those who ask Him! "Beware of the false prophets, who come to you in sheep's clothing,

but <u>inwardly</u> are ravenous wolves.

"You will know them by their fruits."

Many quote this, pretending to know what it is talking about, and having the ability to discern wolves, when it says it is inward wickedness, but lets read on.

"Grapes are not gathered from thorn bushes nor figs from thistles, are they?

"So every good tree bears good fruit, but the bad tree bears bad fruit.

"A good tree <u>cannot</u> produce bad fruit, nor can a bad tree produce good fruit.

"<u>Every</u> tree that does not bear good fruit is cut down

and thrown into the fire.

"So then, YOU WILL KNOW THEM BY THEIR FRUITS."

Here again, talking about trees and inward fruit. It is all inward - inside of you! **Who** will know them? If you can't see the tree is inward, you can't see the fruit either. It is not visible evil that Jesus is talking about here - you must see inside a person. Oprah can see outward fruit, as well as anybody can - that is not a special skill. Do you think she is spiritual?

...And then I will declare to them, 'I never knew you; depart from me, you who PRACTICE LAWLESNESS!"

I want you to key on these words that I am purposely drawing your attention to, because they are the method God ties together themes in scripture to get a picture of what is true concerning a particular subject - like being born again (OR MORE ACCURATELY FROM ABOVE OR OF GOD) or righteousness.

Pay attention to these words as we proceed:
fruit, deeds, good, bad, sin, tree, fire, practice, cannot, evil, born of God, lawlessness, everyone, etc.

THE SCRIPTURE CANNOT BE BROKEN!

I say things to people that set them on edge, like they are evil, and ignorant, and whores. Idiots tell me, **"You need to speak the truth in love,"** as if there is any other way truth can be spoken. A good tree cannot speak that which is evil, and **the mouth of the righteous utters wisdom (Psalm 37:30).** Jesus constantly insulted people and so did the apostles. You are just blind to it.

Here is something wildly offensive. That cute and cuddly baby of yours or someone who you care about, is not innocent - it is an iniquitous evil tree that will grow up to produce a crop of evil fruit seen or unseen by people, but always seen by God and His elect in the invisible realm of the heavens.

Don't you think the terrorists who flew those planes into the twin towers were adorable little Middle Eastern boys at some point in their lives? Of course they were, and they were loved by their mothers and fathers.

That young woman swinging from a stripper pole was daddy's little virginal princess at some time in her past. But that little tender sapling has the DNA inside of it to be completely ABOMINABLE!

"IMPUTED RIGHTEOUSNESS"
WHAT A LOAD OF GARBAGE!

If you are unfamiliar with this teaching, google it like anything else in this book, to get more info. I cannot outline it here with all of its attendant illogical fallacies, that would take 10-15 chapters. This whole idea that you are the "righteousness of God in Christ Jesus" as some stand alone mystical reality when you recite, **"Now I lay me down to sleep, I pray the Lord... to magically make me righteous in Your eyes without any real suffering or proving,"** is LUDRICOUS!

That is another gnat you strain, to the exclusion of the other places in scripture that give the conditions that one must meet in order to claim true righteousness. Stop listening to the liars in the pulpit and on christian TV and read and believe what the scriptures say.
Here is a partial list:

Hebrews 12:5-11 NASB
...and you have forgotten the exhortation which is addressed to you as sons,

"MY SON, DO NOT REGARD LIGHTLY THE DISCIPLINE OF THE LORD,

NOR FAINT WHEN YOU ARE REPROVED BY HIM;

FOR THOSE WHOM THE LORD LOVES HE DISCIPLINES,

AND HE SCOURGES EVERY SON WHOM HE RECEIVES."

It is for discipline that you endure; God deals with you as with sons;

FOR WHAT SON IS THERE WHOM HIS FATHER DOES NOT DISCIPLINE?

But if you are without discipline, of which all have become partakers, then you are **BASTARDS** and **NOT NOT NOT NOT NOT NOT NOT!!! SONS**.

Furthermore, we had earthly fathers to discipline us, and we respected them; shall we not much rather be subject to the Father of spirits, and live?

For they disciplined us for a short time as seemed best to them, but He disciplines us for our good, so that we may share His holiness.

...All discipline for the moment **seems not to be joyful, but sorrowful**; **yet to those who have been trained by it, afterwards it** yields the peaceful **fruit of righteousness.**

You really wanna be righteous, huh? Well, saddle up cowboy and get ready for the wickedness to be burned out of you and the Rod of the Lord's correction to beat it (righteousness) into you! Nobody gets salvation without an incredible ordeal.

1 Peter 4:14-19 NASB
If you are reviled for the name of Christ, you are blessed, because the Spirit of glory and of God rests on you. Make sure that none of you suffers as a murderer, or thief, or evildoer, or a troublesome meddler;

but if anyone ....*suffers as a Christian...*

(*Christian* as only scripture defines *Christian*)

**...he is not to be ashamed,
but is to glorify God in this name...**

Christian is only used twice throughout the entire Greek scriptures - here, as an exhortation to endure mistreatment for bearing the NAME of CHRIST, and as an insult from non-believers in Acts 11:26. Why is the term so prevalent now?

"That man is a good *christian*" - **"Jesus wants *christians* to be blessed and happy!"** or my favorite one that is currently circulating on the internet:

" I AM A CHRISTIAN! "

YET: It only has the connotation of reproach and suffering in the scriptures! **Selah!**

...For it is time for judgment to begin with the household of God; and if it begins with us first, <u>what will be the outcome for those who do not obey the gospel of God</u>? AND IF IT IS **WITH DIFFICULTY** THAT THE RIGHTEOUS IS SAVED, WHAT WILL BECOME OF THE GODLESS MAN AND THE SINNER?

...Therefore, those also **WHO SUFFER ACCORDING TO THE WILL OF GOD** shall entrust their souls to a faithful Creator in doing what is right.

ARE YOU GOING TO MAINTAIN YOUR SILLY POSITION THAT YOU WERE BORN AGAIN AND "SAVED" WHEN YOU SAID A PRAYER THAT SOME LIAR LED YOU IN? **THINK AGAIN:**

1 John 3:4-7 NASB

Everyone who practices sin also practices lawlessness;

AND SIN IS LAWLESSNESS.

You know that He appeared in order to take away sins;

and in Him there is no sin.

No one who abides in Him sins;

NO ONE who sins has seen Him...

OR KNOWS HIM
OR KNOWS HIM
OR KNOWS HIM.

Little children,

<u>MAKE SURE NO ONE DECEIVES YOU</u>;

the one who practices righteousness is righteous, <u>**JUST AS**</u> He is righteous...

Luke 6:40 KJV

The disciple is not above his master: **but every one that is perfect** <u>**shall be as**</u> **HIS MASTER.**

No, that can't be right? **"Christians aren't perfect - just forgiven."** You know seriously, where do people come up with this crap? **"WE ARE JUST SINNERS SAVED BY GRACE."** Grace teaches us to...? **"Ignore our sinfulness and say it is covered by the blood!"**

...the one who practices sin **is of the DEVIL**

If you or anyone you know is in an adulterous remarriage, then according to God's Word, **YOU ARE OF THE DEVIL.** It really doesn't take an overtly wicked person to qualify here.

...for the devil has sinned from the beginning The Son of God appeared for this purpose, to destroy the works of the devil.

No one who is born of God practices sin, because...

His seed abides in him;

and and and and and...
he CANNOT sin,
because he is
born of God.
...By this the children of God and the children of the devil are OBVIOUS.

Again...obvious to whom? I have talked to christians who cannot see the wickedness people are committing. They are blind. Only those who can see <u>inwardly</u> can make this determination. Christian churches have no one in their membership who is truly born of God, because if they claimed to be sinless they would be thrown out as a heretic!

The passage above is so easily dismissed as not being accurate, even though the very words in it (**cannot sin** - or more literally accurate - **IS NOT ABLE TO SIN!**) are undisputed from the Greek text. Without the ability to sin? That scares religious people - to say that you could be sinless, would make you out to be something that is not possible according to the prevailing notion that, as long as we are in this flesh, we will carry out sinful deeds. You are ignoring a mountain of scripture that outlines true transformation from one type of tree to another type of tree.

...anyone who does not practice righteousness
is not of God,
nor the one who does not love his brother.

Last time I checked practice is a verb. You must practice (bear fruit) - but it doesn't look like Oprah's type of good works, nor mother Teresa's. It looks like the Son of God, and what He practiced. His righteous deeds made Him hated.

JOHN 7:7 NASB

The world cannot hate you, **but it hates Me because I testify, testify, testify of it, that its deeds are evil.**

JOHN 5:28-29 NASB

Do not marvel at this; for an hour is coming, in which all who are in the tombs will hear His voice, and will come forth; those who did the good deeds to a resurrection of life, **those who committed the evil deeds to a resurrection of judgment.**

JOHN 3:20 NASB

For <u>EVERYONE WHO DOES EVIL HATES THE LIGHT,</u> and does not come to the Light for fear that his deeds will be exposed.

Just in case they missed it in chapter 3, John had the presence of mind to repeat it in chapter 5.

1 John 5:17-19 NASB

All unrighteousness is sin,
and there is a sin not leading to death.
We know that **no one who is born of God sins;**
but He who was born of God keeps him,
and the evil one does not touch him.
We know that we are of God, and
that the whole world lies in the power of the evil one.

I spent way too much time arguing with what can only be described as a retarded person, who had the most convoluted hermeneutical formula for explaining away this statement in verse 18.

You are gonna have to abandon the whole born again fallacy, that *"You can be born again and MUST still be sinful."* There is no example of anyone who claimed to be born from above in any text in Acts immediately after Pentecost.

Acts 9:1 NASB
The Conversion of Saul
Now Saul, still breathing threats and murder against the disciples of the Lord...

The *conversion* of Saul, huh? Says who?

The liars of the circumcision with their magic lying pen? That heading does not appear in any Greek manuscript, but it is the prevailing doctrine (which happens to be false), that Saul (later Paul), was converted or born from above on the road to Damascus. Really, that is just wild speculation. There is not one iota of textual support to make that case. It is only assumed, and *taken from TRADITIONAL understanding*. Being born from above happened long after Paul had a visitation in Acts 9.

God says do not add to His Word and they added a big LIE right there at the top of chapter 9 and **WE ALL** fell for it. Read Acts 9 and and prove me wrong. That is a wholly made up doctrine.

Peter wasn't born from above either for many years, and neither was I, when the Lord appeared to me in 1986. I was led in the sinner's prayer and all it did was deceive me into believing the same lie...that I was born again - **not true.** Don't feel bad, I was under the same born again hoax nonsense for years myself. I believed what my rebellious deceiving elders told me, too. But when I actually started seeing these verses and words for the very first time and God gave me real faith to believe them, I came out from under that cloud of delusion.

Just because someone who stands in a pulpit says that you are born again, washed in the blood, and saved - don't make it so! The scriptures decide what it means to be regenerated, converted, or saved, and how it is manifested in the real believer's life. I can't separate sound doctrine and the teaching on righteousness, divorce and adultery. It all fits together.

You must know why it says that they will not ENDURE...

Chapter 5
Sound *and*
Not So sound
Doctrine

2 Timothy 4:3-5 NASB
"For the time will come when they will not endure sound doctrine; but wanting to have their ears tickled, they will accumulate for themselves teachers in accordance to their own desires, and **will turn away their ears from the truth** and will turn aside to myths"

I don't want this to turn into a book filled with a bunch of passages that you can read in your own neglected Bible, but these are needed here. If I thought I could just give the reference and expect that you will read it, I would. One of your main problems is: **You think that you are familiar with your Bible - you aren't. You are blind to the very words on the page, and you don't know that you are blind.**

Revelation 2:16-17 NASB
'So because YOU are lukewarm, and neither hot nor cold, I will spit YOU out of My mouth. **'Because YOU say,**

"I am rich, and have become wealthy, and have need of nothing,"

...and YOU do not know that YOU are wretched and miserable and poor and blind and naked."

Again, the words I want you key on are in bold and underlined. You can begin to see how they fit with one another. I am merely **pointing out these things to you** so that you will no longer be poor, blind, naked...

1 Timothy 4:6-7 NASB
In <u>pointing out these things to the brethren</u>,
you will be a **good servant** of Christ Jesus,
constantly nourished (what are we eating here?)
on the words of the faith
and of *the sound doctrine*
which you have been following.
But have **nothing to do** with **worldly fable**s
fit only for old women On the other hand,
discipline yourself for the purpose of godliness...

2 Timothy 4:2-4 NASB
...**preach the word;** be ready in season and out of season;
reprove, rebuke, exhort,
with great patience and instruction. For the time will come when
<u>THEY WILL NOT ENDURE SOUND DOCTRINE</u>;
but *wanting* to have **their ears tickled**,
they will accumulate for themselves
teachers in accordance to their own *<u>desires</u>*,
and will turn away their ears from the truth
and will turn aside to MYTHS.

Titus 1:9-10 NASB
...holding fast the faithful word which is in accordance with

THE TEACHING,

so that he will be able both to exhort in **sound doctrine**
and to **REFUTE THOSE WHO CONTRADICT**...
For there are **many rebellious men,**
empty talkers and deceivers,
especially those of the circumcision...

Titus 2:1 NASB
But as for you,
speak the things which are fitting for

SOUND DOCTRINE.

Now, both of these themes of sound doctrine and the nature and temperament of a genuine prophet, dovetail into one another. On the day of my wedding about 24 years ago, I asked the Lord to give me a direction for my life. I opened my Bible stuck my finger on the page, and my eyes fell on this passage, which I had never read before:

Ezekiel 2:1-10 NASB

The Prophet's Call
Then He said to me, "Son of man,
stand on your feet that I may speak with you!"

As He spoke to me the Spirit entered me and set me on my feet; and I heard Him speaking to me.

Then He said to me, "Son of man, I am **sending** you to the sons of Israel, **to a rebellious people who have rebelled against Me; they and their fathers have transgressed against Me to this very day**.

"**I am sending you to them who are stubborn and obstinate children**, and you shall say to them, 'Thus says the Lord GOD.' "As for them, **whether they listen or not--for they are a rebellious house**--they will know that a prophet has been among them."

(YOU MAY NOT KNOW IT NOW, BUT I ASSURE YOU THAT SOMEDAY YOU WILL)

THE SCRIPTURE CANNOT BE BROKEN

"And you, son of man, neither fear them nor fear their words, though thistles and thorns are with you and you sit on scorpions; **neither fear their words nor be dismayed at their presence, for they are a rebellious house.**

"But you shall speak My words to them whether they listen or not, for they are rebellious.

"Now you, son of man, listen to what I am speaking to you; **do not be rebellious like that rebellious house. Open your mouth and eat what I am giving you."**

Then I looked, and behold, a hand was extended to me; and lo, **a scroll was in it.**

When He spread it out before me, it was written on the front and back, and written on it were **lamentations, mourning and woe.**

Ezekiel 3:1-3 NASB

Then He said to me, "Son of man, **eat what you find; eat this scroll,** and go, speak to the house of Israel." **So I opened my mouth, and He fed me this scroll.** He said to me, "Son of man, feed your stomach and **FILL YOUR BODY WITH THIS SCROLL** which I am giving you" Then I ate it, and it was **sweet as honey in my mouth.**

COMPARE WITH:

Revelation 10:8-11 NASB

Then the voice which I heard from heaven,
I heard again speaking with me, and saying,
"Go, take the book which is open in the hand of the
angel who stands on the sea and on the land."
So I went to the angel, telling him to give me the little book.
And he said to me,"**Take it and eat it;
it will make your stomach bitter,
but in your mouth it will be sweet as honey."
I took the little book out of the angel's hand and ate it,
and in my mouth it was sweet as honey;
and when I had eaten it, my stomach was made bitter.**
And *THEY (both of them)* said to me,
"**You must prophesy again** concerning many peoples
and nations and tongues and kings."

BACK TO EZEKIEL 3:4-27 NASB

THEN He said to me, **"Son of man,
go to the house of Israel and
speak with My words to them.**

"For you are not being sent to a people of unintelligible speech or difficult language, but to the house of Israel, nor to many peoples of unintelligible speech or difficult language,whose words you cannot understand.

**But I have sent you to them
who <u>should listen</u> to you;
yet the house of Israel
<u>will not be willing to listen to you</u>,
since they are not willing to listen to Me.
Surely the whole house of Israel
is stubborn and obstinate. "**

Holy Whoredom

Behold, I have made your face as hard as their faces and your forehead as hard as their foreheads.

"Like emery **harder than flint I have made your forehead.**

(It would appear that there is a righteous stubbornness, as well as an unrighteous variety being plainly indicated above - so one of us is going to one day be broken beyond remedy!)

Do not be afraid of them or be dismayed before them, though they are a rebellious house." Moreover, He said to me, "Son of man, take into your heart **all My words which I will speak to you and listen closely. "Go to the exiles, to the sons of your people, and speak to them and tell them, whether they listen or not,**

'Thus says the Lord GOD.'"

Then the Spirit lifted me up, and I heard a great rumbling sound behind me, "Blessed be the glory of the LORD in His place."

And I heard the sound of the wings of the living beings touching one another and the sound of the wheels beside them, even a great rumbling sound. So the Spirit lifted me up and took me away; and I went **embittered in the rage of my spirit, and the hand of the LORD was strong on me.** Then I came to the exiles who lived beside the river Chebar at Tel-abib, and I sat there seven days where they were living, **causing consternation among them.**

At the end of seven days the word of the LORD came to me, saying, **"Son of man, I have appointed you a watchman to the house of Israel; whenever you hear a word from My mouth, warn them from Me. "**

When I say to the wicked, 'You will surely die,' and you do not warn him or speak out to warn the wicked from his wicked way that he may live, that wicked man shall die in his iniquity, but his blood I will require at your hand.

"Yet if you have warned the wicked and he does not turn from his wickedness or from his wicked way, he shall die in his iniquity; but you have delivered yourself."

Again, when a righteous man turns away from his righteousness and commits iniquity, and I place an obstacle before him, he will die; since you have not warned him, he shall die in his sin, and his righteous deeds which he has done shall not be remembered; but his blood I will require at your hand. "However, if you have warned the righteous man that the righteous should not sin and he does not sin, he shall surely live because he took warning; and you have delivered yourself."

The hand of the LORD was on me there, and He said to me, "Get up, go out to the plain, and there I will speak to you." So I got up and went out to the plain; and behold, the glory of the LORD was standing there, like the glory which I saw by the river Chebar, and I fell on my face.

The Spirit then entered me and made me stand on my feet, and He spoke with me and said to me, "Go, shut yourself up in your house. "As for you, son of man, **they will put ropes on you and bind you with them so that you cannot go out among them.** "*Moreover,* **I will make your tongue stick to the roof of your mouth so that you will be mute and cannot be a man who rebukes them, for they are a rebellious house.**

"But when I speak to you,
I will open your mouth and you will say to them,

'Thus says the Lord GOD'

He who hears, let him hear;

(having ears to hear) **and he who refuses, let him refuse;** *(no ears to hear)*

FOR THEY ARE A REBELLIOUS HOUSE."

People hate the way that I am constantly repeating things, as if I am doing it for sole purpose of being a nuisance. No, I mirror what God does - repeat the same things over and over again, even though no one seems to listen. How many times do you count the words *rebellious, stubborn, obstinate, or should listen, won't listen, whether they listen or not...*?

You may think, **"Wow! is this guy full of himself or what?"** Listen junior, this wasn't an instantaneous process. This was built into me over many years, after everything that resembled me and my former manner of life was brought to nothing. Then, I was forced into this just 2 years ago by God. Before that, I sat and ate the scroll for myself, BEING MUTE and unable to speak. No Bible college, no wise mentors to aid me, but the Lord opened these things up to me in a much more painful manner than you are getting them now, so be thankful instead of **HARD HEADED AND OBSTINATE**.

I have no earthly desire to do this - tell people the undiluted truth and then be rejected as some kind of pariah. My life is absolutely dismal in its continual loneliness.

I have no delusions of my own importance, like Paul said of himself, **"I am a nobody."** Well, so am I. God tells you Himself that **He chooses the weak and foolish in order to put the wise to shame.**

I can run circles around seminary trained theologians when it comes to the true understanding and interpretation of God's Word, even though they would never admit it. They aren't supposed to, it says they won't, and THE SCRIPTURE CANNOT BE BROKEN. Doesn't the passage concerning the **REBELLIOUS House of Israel** in Ezekiel 2 and 3 sound eerily similar to **"THEY WILL NOT ENDURE SOUND DOCTRINE"**?

You might be asking, **"What does all this have to do with sound doctrine?"** More than you might expect. When most people think of doctrine being **SOUND,** they think in terms of it being right or accurate, or true as opposed to false. That is not the main emphasis, even though sound doctrine will always be true.

<u>**The key I want you to understand is this**</u>:
It isn't sound *doctrines* with an "s" - a collection of proper teachings that line up with the truth of God's Word. NOR IS IT DOCTRINE THAT WILL MAKE YOU SICK! Now without ever looking the Greek word up until just now, I knew what it meant because the Lord told me. It means WHOLE, OR HEALTHY, another old English word, "I Believer X, being of sound mind and body, do bequeath unto...".

Isaiah 1:5-7 NASB
Where will you be stricken again,
As you continue in your rebellion?
The whole head is sick And the whole heart is faint.
*From the **<u>SOLE OF THE FOOT EVEN TO THE HEAD</u>***
There is NOTHING SOUND in it,
Only bruises, welts and raw wounds,
 Not pressed out or bandaged, Nor softened with oil.
Your land is desolate, Your cities are burned with fire,
Your fields--strangers are devouring them in your presence;
It is desolation, as overthrown by strangers.

This is a picture of your sickly, diseased "body of Christ"... **There is NO sound doctrine in it whatsoever!** Sound doctrine is **ALSO SINGULAR.** It is contrasted with the plural form found in verses indicating error:

Mark 7:7 NASB
"BUT IN VAIN DO THEY WORSHIP ME,
TEACHING AS *DOCTRINES* THE *PRECEPTS* OF MEN."

…thus observing the *TRADITIONS* of the elders …

1 Timothy 1:3-4 NASB

As I urged you upon my departure for Macedonia, remain on at Ephesus so that you may instruct certain men not to teach *STRANGE DOCTRINES DOCTRINES DOCTRINES*, nor to **pay attention** to *MYTHS* and endless genealogies, which give rise to **mere speculation** rather than furthering the administration of God which is by faith.

1 Timothy 4:1 NASB

But the Spirit explicitly says that in later times some will fall away from the faith, **paying attention** to deceitful spirits and <u>*DOCTRINES DOCTRINES DOCTRINES DOCTRINES*</u>
OF DEMONS...

Here again, we see that word **"myths"** making an appearance. I think most protestants would agree that the idea of many catholic teachings are purely mythological, but what did I say earlier? Isn't God clever enough to be able to make you fall under the spell of something else that keeps you subject to the truth of Ecclesiastes 1? I'm going to upset your apple cart and say something that will be difficult to accept.

Virtually everything in mainstream christianity is false and based on mythology, which is COMPLETELY DEMONIC AT IT'S CORE!

I won't give you even one example because you are not worthy of God's mysteries, and you would only think me mad, because I can't possibly go into the needed detail in order to refute all of your **precious myths and fanciful stories**. Think of the diversity and disparity found in the many opinions in the church.

Once saved always saved, or can you lose your salvation? Freewill or predestination? Women pastors allowed, or men only? Water Baptism - dunked or sprinkled, infant or adult, Jesus' name or Father-Son-Holy Spirit, essential for salvation or only symbolic?

Those are but a few of the fragmented teachings of men. Is it then your job to align yourself with the opinions that most closely mirror yours? That is nonsense - christians can't agree on anything across the board in matters of faith and practice, so they say meaningless things like:

"In essentials, Unity; In non-essentials, Liberty; In all things, Love."

I'd like to know who made these people the arbiters of what is essential and what is non-essential. If you will be a true prophet, then you must eat the whole scroll. That is the entirety of God's Word. As it settles into you, it becomes more and more evident that it is not something that will be pleasant.

Jesus said, "You will be hated by ALL men," but liars like Joel Osteen, T.D. Jakes, and Billy Graham are loved by MANY godless secular leaders and given honor and praise. Do you remember this verse from the last chapter?

Matthew 7:16 NASB
"You will know them by their *fruits.*
Grapes are not *gathered* from *thorn* bushes
nor *figs* from *thistles,* are they?"

Jesus was giving you the key words that you need to make sense out of what He was talking about here, but the word must be so deeply embedded into you by obedience to it and suffering for it. I said before, I have searched the land looking for a godly man and I have never found one.

Holy Whoredom

Matthew 7:16 NASB

"You will know them by their **fruits**. **Grapes** are not **gathered** from **thorn** bushes nor **figs** from **thistles,** are they?"

Cross references:

A. Matthew 7:16 : Matt 7:20; 12:33; Luke 6:44; James 3:12

I pulled the above cross references from the Bible Gateway website in order to demonstrate that the heavenly mind of Christ is more effective than the most hyper-sophisticated computer cross-referencing program, when it comes to unlocking God's veiled mysteries. Look at this passage to understand that Jesus was only giving you the readers digest version in Matthew 7:16. None of the above cross references for Matthew 7 led me to this:

Micah 7:1-4 NASB (The Prophet Acknowledges)

Woe is me!

For I am like the **FRUIT** pickers,

like the **GRAPE GATHERERS.**

There is not a cluster of **GRAPES** to eat,

Or a first-ripe FIG Which I crave.

The godly person has perished from the land,

And there is **no upright person among men.**

All of them lie in wait for bloodshed;

Each of them hunts the other with a net.

Concerning evil, both hands do it well.

The prince asks, also the judge, for a bribe,

And a great man speaks the desire of his soul;

So they weave it together.

THE **BEST** OF THEM IS LIKE A **BRIAR,**
The **MOST UPRIGHT** like a **THORN HEDGE.**

Believer X

Did you catch it? **Fruit, grapes, gathers, figs, thorns, briars...**

Who is looking for figs and grapes among briars and thorns? There aren't many of us. Paul was one:

Galatians 1 and 2 NASB

2:2b; but I did so in private to those **who were of reputation,** for fear that I might be running, or had run, in vain... But from those who were of high reputation (what they were makes no difference to me; God shows no partiality)--**well, those who were of reputation contributed nothing to me.**

Sounds like Peter, James, and John were nothing but a bunch of briars and thorn hedges! The best of them!

...and recognizing the grace that had been given to me,
James and Cephas and John, who were **reputed to be pillars,**
(the best of them - high reputation)...
...gave to me and Barnabas the right hand of fellowship, But when Cephas(Peter) came to Antioch, I opposed him to his face, because he

stood condemned.

Read the rest for yourself and see that Peter was sinning! **Practicing sin, OF THE DEVIL!** Not born from above yet! Ever wonder why it took over 20 years from the time of Pentecost in about 29 A.D., until the first scriptures in the **"New Testament"** were even penned in about 50 A.D.? None of the original twelve apostles were **approved of God** to write His words - they hadn't been through their test that **refined them as pure gold.**

They were still in the **circumcision.** They had no **nourishing sound doctrine** (food, fruit, grapes, figs) to offer Paul when he showed up. That is why Paul wrote most of the Greek scriptures long before Peter was even ready to. Peter spent over 20 years in the false gospel (the circumcision), too.

Have you noticed that I don't use the term **"New Testament"**? **There is a reason - there is no New Testament, there is no Old Testament.**

Holy Whoredom

There are only the scriptures: Hebrew (Law and Prophets) and Greek (Gospels and Epistles), as one seamless revelation from God. They are all the same in quality and substance. O.T. and N.T. is just another trick from the lying pen of the scribes! The new covenant isn't confined to the "new testament" scriptures, and the old covenant isn't confined to the "old testament" scriptures. You are still in the old covenant, until you are in Christ and you must die in Him. It isn't only the law of Moses.

I spent over 20 years going from field to field (CHURCH TO CHURCH), looking to satisfy my soul, and came up with only evil briars and thorns, God-hating christian ministers who will not listen to God's truth. I didn't realize that all of my fruit gathering efforts in the church would be in vain.

Betrayed and broken, He poured His counsel into me and showed me what truth is, without the benefit of much more than some Greek and Hebrew reference books, interlinear Greek and Hebrew Bibles, and a handful of translations. I don't use any Bible computer program - I look up the verses that are already burned into my brain on Bible Gateway. Now it is your turn. Will you believe, or will you stubbornly cling to your traditions that keep you on the broad road leading to destruction? If you are thirsty, I will give you the water of life.

I will close out this chapter with an illustration. Think of sound doctrine as the internal combustion engine in your car that has many parts and systems. It is really a technological marvel, everything linked together working simultaneously and contained in a single contraption, that makes our car take us where we want to go.

Now, all of those hundreds of parts make up the whole engine. If you've never studied it, I won't bore you with the details, but it only takes one thing wrong with it, in order for your car to not run, and it doesn't even have to be something major - **"essential"**.

Sound doctrine has no error in it - it is healthy and whole. Like a brand new car right off of the showroom floor. Each part is dependent on the other part's soundness. If you do not have sound doctrine, your whole theology is messed up. There are no "non-essential" doctrines...

There is only THE Doctrine OR TEACHING

of Christ, depending on which translation you use. It is the same Greek word, but God has purposely ordained all of these lying translations in order to create confusion and error. ***Babylon*** means confusion. Don't all the opinions swirling about like a vortex of uncertainty in christianity make you ever wonder about Jesus' promise to lead us into ALL TRUTH? It did me! Doesn't the following lend itself to confusion?

2 John 1:9 KJV
Whosoever **transgresseth**, and abideth not in **THE DOCTRINE** of Christ, hath not God. He that abideth in **THE DOCTRINE** of Christ, he hath both the Father and the Son.

NASB
Anyone who **goes <u>too far</u> and does not abide in THE TEACHING of Christ, does not have God;** the one **who abides in THE TEACHING, he has both the Father and the Son.**

Do you really believe that wreck of miscellaneous teachings (that you are continually going to the junk yard to replace with more worn out false teachings from some huckster in a leisure suit at your corner synagogue of Satan), is **SOUND DOCTRINE** and **THE TEACHING OF CHRIST?** NOT EVEN CLOSE!

We are still in kindergarten boys and girls, **THE TEACHING OF CHRIST** is only the first aspect of apostolic revelation but you must accept the truth concerning remarriage being adultery first because the foundation is built using truth.

Hebrews 6:1-2 KJV
Therefore **leaving the principles of THE DOCTRINE of Christ, let us go on unto perfection**; **not laying again the (ONE - single) foundation** of repentance from dead works, **and** of faith toward God, Of the **doctrine** of baptisms, **and** of laying on of hands, **and** of resurrection of the dead, **and** of eternal judgment.

Not six separate foundational *doctrines* - ONE single... unified *TEACHING* encompassing **just the basics**! You have not learned any correct or sound doctrine if you have drawn from the Babylonian whore's poisoned well of lies and sewage!

Holy Whoredom

Do you see a pattern beginning to develop here? With **SOUND DOCTRINE,** you have uniformity, cohesion, and correlation between subjects and words. They fit together like a puzzle, and aren't fraught with endless contradictions and inconsistencies.

...And this will we do, **if God permit.**

But God doesn't permit me to go beyond the premise in this book. Do you see the monumental task that I am confronted with? I have to write this huge book in order for you to accept just a handful of verses about the permanence of marriage. I can't possibly address the error contained in the multitude of heresies in the vile christian abomination.

This is just a primer to get you to purify and separate yourself from...

Chapter 6
The Circumcision

A.K.A. – The Great Whore, The false circumcision, Scribes, Pharisees and Lawyers, Baal's prophets, Princes of Israel, Jerusalem, Sodom, The Synagogue of Satan, or just about any derogatory label in scripture is aimed directly at your rebellious pastors and prophets that prophesy vanity in the christian church, as well as those who FOOLISHLY hearken to them.

Philippians 3:1-3 NASB
Finally, my brethren, rejoice in the Lord.
To write the same things again (and again and again?) is no trouble to me, **and it is a safeguard for you.**
BEWARE of the **DOGS,**
BEWARE of the **EVIL WORKERS,**
BEWARE of the *FALSE* **CIRCUMCISION**;
for **WE** are the **TRUE CIRCUMCISION,**
who worship in the Spirit of God and glory in Christ Jesus
and **PUT NO CONFIDENCE IN THE FLESH...**

Before you start to think to yourself, *"it says, 'we are the true circumcision', so that must mean me"* (meaning you). Not so fast Quick-draw, Paul told the carnal Corinthians that **"WE have the mind of Christ"** - NOT YOU.

A vile woman pastor (**SPACEY-TRACY HASKELL**) told my wife that she (my wife) had the mind of Christ, right before she filed for divorce. No, Paul had the mind of Christ. He was the true circumcision. I have the mind of Christ, I am the true circumcision.

You, I am not so sure about, but probably not. **If you are not receiving the Word of God with meekness and humility, then your soul is *not* being saved.** You cannot claim scriptures for yourself, if the witness of scripture regarding that subject is not completed in you. What is to stop someone like Hitler from saying he is the true circumcision, if all you have to do is read something and claim it for yourself?

Let me tell you something about being born from above. If there is anything in scripture that mirrors the natural, it is this. How much influence did you contribute to your being born the first time? Did you ever say, or hear your children ever say *"I didn't ask to be born!"* Well, I didn't ask to be born from above - I was involuntarily pushed down the restrictive, confining, suffocating, claustrophobic birth canal of the free woman. You don't decide to **"get saved"** on your own or become the elect of your own volition.

The last part of this statement (verse 13) is rarely ever quoted:

John 1:12-13 NASB

But as many as received Him,

to them He gave the right to become children of God,

even to those who believe in His name,

who were **born...**

not of blood...

nor of the **will of the flesh...**

nor of the **will of man...**

but of God.

You were not even aware of what sound doctrine was, which is the foundation. How could you have the **FOUNDATION,** if NOBODY in *YOUR* church even knows what it is? If you reject the premise contained in the previous chapter, then this is going to be a meaningless endeavor on my part.

1 Corinthians 3:9-11 NASB
For **WE** are God's fellow workers; **YOU** are God's field...

(Even though you are filled with worthless weeds, briars and thorn hedges. I have a lot of brush clearing to do)

...and God's building. According to the grace of God which was given to me, like a wise master builder I **laid a foundation,** and another is building on it. But each man must be careful how he builds on it. **For no man can lay a FOUNDATION other than the one which is laid, WHICH IS JESUS CHRIST.**

But He is and will forever be ... **THE STONE THAT the builders (who labor in vain) will ALWAYS REJECT. Not enduring sound doctrine** is synonymous with the rejection of Christ Himself!!!

I cannot bring you into the upper stories until you are founded on Christ and the **TRUTH OF THE GOSPEL**. It is time to tear down that crooked structure of hay. This means those six aspects of the **TEACHING OF CHRIST** are the order of first things first. This is the apostolic task, **to build you into a spiritual house/temple where Christ can dwell. I labor till Christ is formed in you**.

What you must admit (which is hard I know), is that everything you learned before is worthless and must be incinerated. This is the judgment of God - to destroy the evil tree, so that He may plant the new good tree.

The ones who have come before me did not care about you. They were serpents and wolves. I want to point out their hypocrisy and wickedness, and I will use Peter as the prime example to show you that even he was not immune to the bewitching spell of the false circumcision.

Here goes the word game:

beware, hypocrisy, teaching, many, few, leaven, bondage, truth of the gospel, false brethren, circumcision...

Peter was Jesus' closest disciple, right? He was the first pope (hah!). Jesus designated Peter as the undisputed leader of His church right?

UPON THIS ROCK I I I I I I I WILL BUILD MY MY MY MY MY MY MY CHURCH...

But you have only a theory as to when that occurred, based on what you think is true. It will go much easier if you look at this without any assumptions that what you have been taught before now has any validity.

I will show you that it doesn't...

Matthew 16:6-12 NASB
And Jesus said to them,

"Watch out and beware
of the **leaven of the Pharisees** and Sadducees."

They began to discuss this among themselves, saying, "He said that because we did not bring any bread."

But Jesus, aware of this, said, "You men of little faith, why do you discuss among yourselves that you have no bread?

"Do you not yet understand or remember the five loaves of the five thousand, and how many baskets full you picked up?

"Or the seven loaves of the four thousand, and how many large baskets full you picked up?

"How is it that you do not understand that I did not speak to you concerning bread? But **beware of the leaven of the Pharisees and Sadducees.**"

Then they understood that He **did not say to beware of the leaven of bread,** but of the **teaching of the Pharisees and Sadducees**.

Mark 8:14-16 NASB

And they had forgotten to take bread, and did not have more than one loaf in the boat with them.

And He was giving orders to them, saying,

"Watch out!

<u>Beware</u> of the **leaven** of the Pharisees and the **leaven of Herod.**"

They began to discuss with one another the fact that they had no bread.

Luke 12:1 NASB

Under these circumstances, after so many thousands of people had gathered together that they were stepping on one another, He began saying to His disciples,

"First of all, first of all, first of all, <u>Beware</u> of the **leaven** of the Pharisees, which is <u>hypocrisy</u>.

Philippians 3:2
BEWARE of the dogs,
BEWARE of the evil workers,
BEWARE!!! of the
...FALSE CIRCUMCISION...

Three **bewares** in the gospels and three **bewares** in Philippians - it is the infecting influence of leaven that corrupts even the most zealous disciple. You must see the correlation between the Pharisees and the false circumcision. I need to give you a timeline of events. This will be brief, but you need to see how this all plays out in the principle of **"THAT WHICH HAS BEEN IS THAT WHICH WILL BE."**

Jesus gave Peter and the other disciples those warnings in about 27 A.D. or so. Beware of hypocrisy and false teaching of the Pharisees and Herod (wasn't Herod committing adultery?... hmmm...).

Now skip ahead to somewhere about 20 or so years later. Peter is in Jerusalem and the church has grown considerably.

There are now non-Jewish believers (Gentiles) who are part of the church. There are strict proponents of the law of Moses who believe the Gentiles are some sort of sub species of believer. They don't eat with these Gentiles. They are, after all, the chosen people of God. This is at the heart of their teaching ritualistic observance of ceremony and nationalism (God bless America - the christian nation! - **WRETCHING SOUND!**).

Peter is overcome by the leaven on two counts: hypocrisy and false teaching, that Jesus told him to beware of over 20 years prior to that. We can clearly see this in Galatians 2 below, but I want you you look at the phrases that give a solid timeline to set the stage first. Start with 3 and 1/2 years - the length of Jesus' ministry when He called Peter "the Rock", Circa 26 A.D.- 29 A.D.

Galatians 1:15-18 NASB

But when it pleased God, who separated me from my mother's womb...I did not immediately confer with flesh and blood, nor did I go up to Jerusalem to those *WHO WERE* apostles before me; but I went to Arabia, and returned again to Damascus...

Here we have the initial description of Paul's encounter with Christ on the road to Damascus. This could not have been before 30 A.D.

...Then after <u>three years</u> I (Paul) went up to Jerusalem to see Peter, and remained with him fifteen days.

We are up to at least 33 A.D. Following?

Galatians 2:1-18 NASB

Then after an interval of **fourteen years** I went up again to Jerusalem with Barnabas, taking Titus along also...

Now, we add 14 years to 33 A.D., but this is conservative - it is probably 3-5 years later because Paul (as Saul) would have had a church to persecute, that had been growing for at least a few years. We are up to at least 47 A.D. Is there anything wrong with my math? Now, Paul shows up and he has his ministry entourage with him (Titus and Barnabas).

Look what happens next:
...But not even Titus, who was with me, though he was a Greek, **was compelled to be *CIRCUMCISED*.** But it was because of the **FALSE BRETHREN secretly brought in**, who had sneaked in to spy out our liberty which we have in Christ Jesus, **in order to *BRING US INTO BONDAGE*.**
...But
WE DID NOT YIELD IN SUBJECTION TO THEM FOR EVEN AN HOUR,
so that the <u>TRUTH OF THE GOSPEL</u> would remain with you.

Were they successful? Not with Paul, and they are no longer successful with me, **but...**

...But from those who were of **high reputation** (what they were makes no difference to me; God shows no partiality)--well, those who were of **reputation contributed nothing to me.**

They did not help Paul stand against the false brethren of the circumcision party. Did you see the connection?

...But on the contrary, seeing that I had been entrusted with the gospel to the uncircumcised, just as Peter had been to the circumcised (for He who effectually worked for Peter in his **apostleship to the circumcised** effectually worked for me also to the Gentiles), and recognizing the grace that had been given to me, **James and Cephas and John,** who were reputed to be pillars... **(I want you to remember this phrase for later.)** ...gave to me and Barnabas the right hand of fellowship, so that we might go to the Gentiles and they to the circumcised. They only asked us to remember the poor--the very thing I also was eager to do.

Peter (Cephas) Opposed by Paul

...But when Cephas came to Antioch, I opposed him to his face, because he stood condemned...

Now we have an indefinite period of time after Paul left Jerusalem when Peter traveled to visit Paul in Antioch about 300 miles away - not a mere days journey.

...**For prior to the coming of certain men from James, he (Peter) used to eat with the Gentiles; but when they came, he began to withdraw and hold himself aloof,**

FEARING, FEARING, FEARING, FEARING, THE PARTY OF THE CIRCUMCISION.

After 20 plus years of being **"born again"** (according to your worthless theory), how could "the Rock" be fearing false brethren and sinning? **Are hypocrisy and cowardice not SINS?**

...**The rest of the Jews joined him in hypocrisy, with the result that even Barnabas was carried away by their hypocrisy.**

So, here we have Barnabas falling into the **sin of HYPOCRISY** after he and Paul separated. Barnabas was still carnal and would not submit to Paul's apostolic authority. This was the consequence of not listening to Paul, **who was never wrong**.

...But when **I saw that *they were not* straightforward about the truth of the gospel,** I said to Cephas in the presence of all, "If you, being a Jew, live like the Gentiles and not like the Jews, how is it that you compel the Gentiles to live like Jews? "**We are Jews by nature and not sinners** from among the Gentiles; nevertheless knowing that a man is not justified by the works of the Law but through faith in Christ Jesus, even we have believed in Christ Jesus, so that we may be justified by faith in Christ and not by the works of the Law; since by the works of the Law no flesh will be justified. "**But if, while seeking to be justified in Christ, we ourselves have also been found sinners, is Christ then a minister of sin? May it never be!** "For if I **REBUILD** what I have **once destroyed**, I prove myself to be a transgressor."

You must understand that this was not some minor lapse in judgment, as most would have you believe. This was Peter totally overcome with idolatry and leaven, which Jesus had told him to **beware of, at least 3 times**. The woman (Jezebel) taught Christ's bond-servant (Peter) to commit acts of fornication and to eat things sacrificed to idols.

Jesus led Peter into the false gospel for the very purpose of bringing him out of it. The circumcision and the tares are the same. Tares are those who use Biblical terminology stripped of the real meaning that the scriptures provide (the context of what things like grace, salvation, and true faith really are). Tares just spout a bunch of empty phrases that anyone can claim for themselves without actually having to demonstrate some good fruit.

Now, Paul began writing the scriptures right about this time (47-50 A.D.), but Peter did not pen his two letters until sometime after 60 A.D., at the earliest, according to what can be deduced. He was very far behind Paul in the gospel, even though he walked with Jesus in his earthly ministry. It doesn't help to know Christ after the flesh, it actually hinders you.

Holy Whoredom

Peter had a carnal mindset, so he did not receive the gospel by revelation (spiritual understanding). He received it from Paul's preaching and was approved of God much later.

So, when you understand Christ's words of reproof in Revelation chapters 2-3, **they all applied to Peter.** He was disciplined by the Lord through Paul's apostolic ministry. This must have been rather humbling for Peter to submit to the new kid on the block.

There are only two ways available for you to receive the gospel - either you get it by a direct revelation of Jesus Christ, like Paul and I did, or you receive it from one whom Christ **sends** - one of his GENUINE Apostles.

Maybe now is a good time to give an accurate depiction of an Apostle. He is not some grandiose famous evangelist or popular TV preacher. He is, like his **MASTER,** hated and rejected by all but a few. If I give you the reference, will you please read it?

1 Corinthians 4 NASB

Servants of only Christ, **faithful** stewards of Gods mysteries, mistreated, slandered, dishonored, condemned to death, last, fools, a father of wayward children in the faith, etc...

You are in need of the **truth of the gospel,** which is the Word of God, without all of the trappings and hoops that evil men would have you jump through. **Circumcision is a metaphor for things that have no value in the faith.**

Wedged firmly in the middle of the marriage chapter in
1 Corinthians 7 we find this statement:

Circumcision is.............. NOTHING,

and uncircumcision is................... NOTHING,

but WHAT MATTERS is the

KEEPING OF THE COMMANDMENTS OF GOD.

Until you realize that this marriage teaching is crucial to your evidencing a genuine **OBEDIENCE OF FAITH** to God and Christ, then you will be in rebellion and under God's harsh sentence of condemnation. You can sing your vain "worship" songs for hours and God doesn't regard it even the least little bit. Those tithes and "love offerings" you are manipulated into giving don't garner you any favor with God either.

If you are following the majority, then you are ignoring a main premise that is found *EVERYWHERE* in the Bible.

2 Corinthians 2:17 NASB

For we are not like many,...

peddling (KAPELEUO)...

Definition from The NASB New Testament Greek Lexicon

1. to be a retailer(this is an exorbitant mark-up from a free gospel to the bait and switch of OVERPRICED LIES), to peddle
2. to make money by selling anything
    a. to get **SORDID GAIN** by dealing in anything, to do a thing for base gain
    b. to trade in the word of God
        a. to try to get base gain by teaching divine truth
    c. to **CORRUPT, TO ADULTERATE**
        a. peddlers were in the habit of adulterating their commodities for the sake of gain

...the word of God, but as from sincerity, but as from God, we speak in Christ in the sight of God.

I am about as "few" as you can get. Nobody else teaching out of the Bible agrees with me. YET, EVERYONE uses this verse to say they are among the few that don't fall into the many, while they have the same worn out majority opinions.

God's servants and faithful stewards have unique information that cannot be found anywhere else. Even among those who teach the permanence of marriage, I part company on most of what they teach, because they think for the most part, that christianity is just deceived in the MDR area. Not so! I already mentioned the old wine, let's look at the pertinent text:

Luke 5:36-39 NASB

And He was also telling them a parable: "No one tears a piece of cloth from a new garment and puts it on an old garment; otherwise he will both tear the new, and the piece from the new will not match the old.

"And no one puts new wine into old wineskins; otherwise the new wine will burst the skins and it will be spilled out, and the skins will be ruined.

"But new wine must be put into fresh wineskins. **"And no one, after drinking old wine wishes for new; for he says, 'The old is good enough.'"**

How many times will I have to repeat this before it sinks in?

THAT WHICH HAS BEEN IS THAT WHICH WILL BE...NO REMEMBRANCE!

This is a *parable,* (you are not worthy of a full explanation), but I do want you to notice something at the end. Verse 39 says:

No one,... *after drinking old wine...*
WISHES FOR NEW.
NO ONE WISHES FOR THE NEW.

Are you going to call Jesus a liar and insist that you want His new wine OR THAT THE MASSES IN CHRISTENDOM WILL WISH FOR IT? **He says without any doubt, that neither YOU, NOR THEY will wish for it!** You will not want the gospel of truth, because it is 180 degrees from your **TRADITIONS AND ABOMINATIONS** that you are stubbornly clinging to.

Do you really believe this is talking about the Jewish religion that is observed today? You must OVERCOME the desire to drink yourself into a stupor with the old wine of christianity, that uses all of those empty terms of the Bible in the **"New Testament."**

Jesus does the same thing with all of His bond-servants whom He calls. He throws them into the snake den of the evil workers - they are treated shamefully and subsequently Christ reveals the truth to them during their trial. That is what happened to me.

I was absolutely mystified as to why the christians who knew me and my wife would not tell her to stop her unbridled evil toward me. It is just so plainly written in the Bible that what she was doing was wrong and sinful.

I didn't commit adultery or fornication, I didn't leave home, I was not beating her. She just wanted to be "HAPPY" because that is what God wanted for her, and I wasn't making her happy, even though I tried. Her love grew cold because of the increasing lawlessness in the "church" Jesus said would be the reason. I talked and counseled with pastors and ministers of the "gospel" and none of them would lift a finger to help me.

So, after more than 20 years together, and 2 children whom I have not seen in over 5 long years, she divorced me. I didn't sign any of the divorce papers - I told the judge (who most likely took his oath of office with his hand on a Bible) that he had neither the authority, nor the ability to dissolve my marriage. Well, he thought I was unbalanced and ordered me to take a lethality test which I was to pay for. I didn't take it, and about 1 month later my marriage was declared over by the state of Colorado. But that was just the beginning of my wife's **UNRIGHTEOUS TREACHERY AND WICKEDNESS.**

This isn't about my personal tragedy. If it was, there would be a lot more details I could easily share. This is about the blindness of those who claim Christ's Lordship, but ignore basic truths found in the writings of scripture. If you think I am solely motivated by anger and hurt, that is not the case. I don't care if you believe me or not. It would be nice, but I am only called to preach, and the results, positive or negative, are at God's discretion.

It was the circumstances of my life that brought my attention to the real meaning of Titus 1, which I had never seen before. **THE EVIL WORKERS** and **THE DOGS** and the proponents of ANOTHER gospel - **THE FALSE CIRCUMCISION not being straightforward about the truth** caused...

MY FAMILY TO BE TORN APART (SUBVERTED - UPSET), WHILE THEY STRENGTHENED MY WIFE'S HANDS TO DO EVIL TO HER COVENANT HUSBAND, AND THEREBY TURNED HER INTO A WHORE!

I am not the only person this has happened to, and we are in the silent and oppressed minority. **God says He will avenge those who are being defrauded,** but most who fall victim to no-fault divorce never come to the knowledge of the truth. They do what they are foolishly advised to do... *"Move on, remarry, salvage what is left of your life, put up with egregious custody arrangements. God doesn't want you to be unhappy,"* and all of the other meaningless platitudes and lies that have zero basis in scripture.

Well, that wasn't gonna work for me because I already had Ezekiel's vision of God's glory on March 11 of 1986. There was never going to be any way I would forget that. I knew that I was going to suffer early on, but I never imagined in my worst nightmare that it would be from the sweet christian godly woman that I thought I was marrying - I just assumed that it would be deep in the jungle of the mission field at the hands of mud worshiping tribesmen.

The scriptures had to be fulfilled in me, too. I had to be taught those same vile lies and abominations of Jezebel. I was His bondservant...

THE SCRIPTURE CANNOT BE BROKEN...
I had to be taught error by Jezebel.

What is interesting is the speed at which God revealed all these things to me. I started waking up from my night of drunken debauchery with Leah only a few years ago. He began to undo all of the lies at lightning speed. I could teach anyone who is willing to **listen,** more in a single afternoon than what they could learn in twenty years of **"going to church"** three times a week.

My sweet old baptist grandma spent her life in the "church" and died never having truly overcome. Instead of becoming the tree of righteousness, she became more nasty and iniquitous as she approached death. That is the fruit of the evil tree whose end is death.

James 1:14-16 NASB

But each one is tempted when he is carried away and enticed by his own lust. Then when lust has conceived, it gives birth to sin; and when sin is accomplished, (fully mature - fruit bearing) it brings forth death. (This is that wicked tree that must die, so that it can no longer bear fruit for death in the true believer's life)

Do not be deceived, my beloved brethren.

Romans 7:4-5 NASB

Therefore, my brethren, **YOU ALSO WERE MADE TO DIE** to the Law through the body of Christ, so that you might be joined to another, to Him who was raised from the dead, in order that we might bear fruit for God. For while we were in the flesh, the sinful passions, **WHICH WERE AROUSED BY THE LAW**, were at work in the members of our body

TO BEAR FRUIT FOR DEATH.

I can't go into very much detail, and I am sure I will be accused of **"QUOTING THINGS OUT OF CONTEXT, MIS-APPLICATION, AND BLAH BLAH BLAH."** But look at the **WORDS!**

Romans 6:19-23 NASB

I am speaking in human terms because of the

WEAKNESS OF YOUR FLESH

For just as you presented your members as

SLAVES TO IMPURITY AND TO LAWLESSNESS,

resulting in further lawlessness,

so now present your members as

slaves to righteousness, resulting in sanctification.

For **when** you were ***SLAVES OF SIN,***
you were free in regard to righteousness.
Therefore what **benefit (lit. FRUIT!)** were you then deriving from the things of which you are **now ashamed?**
For the **outcome of those things is death.**
But now having been **freed from sin and enslaved to God,**
you derive your **benefit (again lit. FRUIT),**
resulting in sanctification, and the outcome, **eternal life.**
For the wages of sin is death, but...

(This is a BIG LIE - the word in the Greek is more properly translated "AND". It is silly to imply something that many other texts flatly deny - that everyone does not merit death as the wages for their sin!)

...the free gift of God is **eternal life** in Christ Jesus our Lord.

The empty talk of the tares and their ilk will tell you goofy things like...

"You can't live above sin"

WHY NOT? If you are truly **FREED FROM AND DEAD TO SIN, AND ENSLAVED TO GOD** as the text says? This kind of error only leads to a **grace of licentiousness *(unbridled lust)*** that excuses sin. It is the inevitable consequence of this **false teaching** that is in direct contradiction to the truth contained in the phrases of Romans above.

This is the reason why your church is a brothel filled with covenant-breaking whores and whore-mongers. **If you believe the "LORD" is in your midst, then you are sadly mistaken.**

Believer X

**He has taken away your lamp stand -
the light of His truth,
and you are groping around in the darkness...**

STICKING YOUR GENITALS IN PLACES YOU OUGHT NOT!

Again this is in no way comprehensive in its scope, but if I don't move on this book will be 1,000 pages.

Chapter 7
The "church" or THE CHURCH – That Depends On Your Auditory Ability

Revelation 2 and 3 NASB

He who has an ear,

<u>LET HIM HEAR</u> what the Spirit says to **the churches** (this phrase is repeated 7 times)

<u>To him who overcomes,</u> (repeated X 7 AGAIN!)

and he who <u>keeps</u> My deeds <u>until the end</u>,

1. I will grant to eat of the tree of life which is in the Paradise of God;
2. will not be hurt by the second death;
3. I will give some of the hidden manna;
4. and I will give him a white stone;
5. and a new name written on the stone which no one knows but he who receives it;
6. TO HIM I WILL GIVE AUTHORITY OVER THE NATIONS;

Believer X

7. AND HE SHALL RULE THEM WITH A ROD OF IRON, AS THE VESSELS OF THE POTTER ARE BROKEN TO PIECES, as I also have received authority from My Father;
8. and I will give him the morning star;
9. will thus be clothed in white garments;
10. and I will not erase his name from the book of life;
11. and I will confess his name before My Father;
12. and before His angels;
13. I will make him a **pillar (remember Peter was reputed to be a pillar)** in the temple of My God;
14. and he will not go out from it anymore;
15. and I will write on him the name of My God;
16. and the name of the city of My God, the new Jerusalem, which comes down out of heaven from My God;
17. and My new name;
18. I will grant to him to sit down with Me on My throne, as I also overcame and sat down with My Father on His throne;
19. <u>**AND** Be faithful **until death**, and I will give you the crown of life</u>.

WOW, I get all that by saying, **"Jesus, come into my heart and make me brand new, I am truly sorry..."** Wait, that's it...that's all I have to do? What a deal, where do I sign up for that?

SUPREME UNMITIGATED STUPIDITY!

Just how many churches are there? Do you count 7, or is there just one? I am going to propose something that is totally foreign to your thinking. There isn't one **church**. There aren't seven churches. *EVEN IN REVELATION* - there are, in fact, two churches.

What have I been talking about all along? Overcoming the things that are written immediately before the promises.

Holy Whoredom

Jesus says YOU are doing all of these rebellious acts, and then He says IF YOU OVERCOME, you get all of this cool stuff (nineteen things listed in two chapters that have no EARTHLY LITERAL TANGIBLE VALUE!). Not limos and Learjets, like Kenneth Copeland and Benny Hinn would lead you to believe, but true spiritual treasure that you can share with the poor and blind of the world.

Matthew 13:52 NASB
And Jesus said to them, "Therefore **every scribe who has become a disciple of the kingdom of heaven is** like a **head of a household,** who brings out of his **treasure** things new and old."

I have a storehouse of treasure that God has been handing over to me as an initial part of my inheritance, that no one seems to want. This new wine has no display room afforded it in the overpriced and merchandised whore church's vineyard of rotting grapes and bottles of rancid vinegar that date all the way back to the **"glorious reformation".**

THEY WILL NOT ENDURE OR *TOLERATE* SOUND DOCTRINE!

THE SCRIPTURE CANNOT BE BROKEN!

So what do these two churches look like:

Galatians 4:22-31 NASB

For it is written that Abraham had two sons, one by the bondwoman and one by the free woman. **But the son by the bondwoman was born according to the flesh, and the son by the free woman through the promise.** This is **allegorically...**

(This is figuratively, metaphorically - *not* literally. Stop thinking in any visible sensual terms. This is not talking about the natural Jew - this is talking about those in slavery to sin, which is the type of church that remarried adulterers attend.)

...speaking,

for these (2) women are two covenants:

one proceeding from Mount Sinai **bearing children who are to be slaves; she is Hagar.**

Now this Hagar is Mount Sinai in Arabia and corresponds to the **present Jerusalem, for she is in slavery with her children.** But the Jerusalem above is free; she is **our** mother.

For it is written, "REJOICE, BARREN WOMAN WHO DOES NOT BEAR; BREAK FORTH AND SHOUT, YOU WHO ARE NOT IN LABOR; FOR MORE NUMEROUS ARE THE CHILDREN OF THE DESOLATE THAN OF THE ONE WHO HAS A HUSBAND."

And you brethren, like Isaac, are children of promise.

But as at that time he who was born according to the flesh persecuted him who was born according to the Spirit, so it is now also. But what does the Scripture say? "CAST OUT THE BONDWOMAN AND HER SON, FOR THE SON OF THE BONDWOMAN SHALL NOT BE AN HEIR WITH THE SON OF THE FREE WOMAN." So then, brethren,

we are not children of a bondwoman, but of the free woman.

Two trees, two sons, two women, two buildings, two temples, two doorposts, two thresholds, two of this and two of that...but ONLY one CHURCH? Think, think, think, think, think, PLEASE! I can't possibly go beyond merely pointing these things out and writing briefly. Peter said that apostles like **Paul wrote things that were hard to understand** and the writer of Hebrews said that they **were hard or difficult to explain.**

Writing is only able to convey so much in a limited way, because of its inability to convey tone and really elaborate with other pertinent texts. That is the reason preaching (speaking) is vital to communicate these things in a more comprehensive fashion.

God explained these things to me by revelation, which is an even higher and more effective type of communication. God spoke to me in bursts, in huge chunks of understanding. That is why an audible voice is so limiting.

God isn't restricted to carnal speech when He speaks by revelation, but the language of revelation is still in thoughts that I can understand and convey in English. It is just much quicker, similar to a download of a huge file into a computer.

I would not want to have to ever rely on the outmoded method of having God explain these things to me by an audible voice that I would have to hear with my natural ears. I am no longer deaf. I have those ears that hear.

Jesus **opened my mind to the Scriptures,** which had been veiled to me for years. I would read through the Bible every six months when I was younger. Now I don't read it at all - in the last four years, I have probably read less than 100 pages in my Bible.

I can't stop **the words of Christ from dwelling within me richly** because I have obeyed those words and died to sin.

James 1:22-25 NASB

But **prove yourselves <u>DOERS</u> of the word,**

and **not merely hearers** who delude themselves.

For if anyone is a hearer of the word and not a doer,

he is like a man who looks at his natural face in a mirror;

for once he has looked at himself and gone away, he has **immediately forgotten what kind of person he was.**

But one who looks intently at the perfect law,

the law of liberty, and **abides** by it,

not having become **a forgetful hearer**

but an effectual **DOER,**

this man will be blessed in what he does.

I had read all of those verses over and over on marriage, and I **"fellowshipped"** with remarried adulterers, whom I thought were **"born again"**, too. The seed of God's Word, which I would never have admitted that I did not possess, could find no good soil to take root in my heart. So, it is not like I haven't had to take the same medicine that I am offering you. Everyone has forsaken me. This is the path of the empty narrow road. Are you willing to join me, and leave the bond woman in the dust, knowing that it will cost you your very life?

I can literally go in a dozen different directions and end up in the same place. That is how the engine of sound doctrine works. Everything is connected and knit together into one cohesive unit.

NOT like this:

Micah 7:2-4 NASB

The godly person has perished from the land,

And there is no upright person among men

All of them lie in wait for bloodshed;

Each of them hunts the other with a net.

Concerning evil, both hands do it well

The prince asks, also the judge, **for a bribe,**

And a great man speaks the desire of his soul;

So they *weave it together.*

The Hebrew is used of intertwining (twisting) cords together. The best of them is like a briar, The most upright like a thorn hedge. The day when you post your watchmen,

Your punishment will come.

Then their (Babylonian) **confusion** will occur.

2 Peter 3:16 CEV
Paul talks about these same things in all his letters, but part of what he says is **hard to understand.**

Some ignorant and unsteady people even destroy themselves by <u>twisting</u> **what he said.** They do the same thing with **other Scriptures too.**

I found at least 5 translations that used the word "twisting". Who is twisting scripture to fit their preconceived traditions that protect their ill-gotten gain from unsuspecting adulterers and adulteresses? I do not blame the stupid sinful sheep nearly as much as I squarely place the blame on the ones who are truly **SUPPRESSING THE TRUTH IN UNRIGHTEOUSNESS.**

Most seminary students who later become pastors are at least aware of the view that marriage is a permanent covenant. They just pick the doctrine that best suits their desire for wealth and popularity. This is what a hireling is, doing it for money and a living, not concerned about the sheep. They compromised their beliefs long before they entered into the ministry. These guys read books and exalt knowledge so they can impress you with their great intellect.

There is a scene in *Good Will Hunting* that illustrates this principle - where Will Hunting (Matt Damon) puts the smarmy rich spoiled college boy to shame with his superior knowledge, that he obtained only from the library and $1.50 in late charges, as opposed to the $150,000 that Mr. Know-It-All paid for his Harvard education.

http://www.youtube.com/watch?v=ymsHLkB8u3s

I learned all of this stuff from a few Bibles and a handful of books that cost me less than 200 bucks 22 years ago. God does not choose the seminary trained spoiled brats of the circumcision to be stewards of His mysteries. He picks some uneducated poor slob like me, who He began to draw at an early age, and then through the circumstance of tremendous injustice, He pours His counsel into him at a time that He designates.

1 Kings 16:29-33 NASB

Now Ahab the son of Omri became king over Israel in the thirty-eighth year of Asa king of Judah, and Ahab the son of Omri reigned over Israel in Samaria twenty-two years.
Ahab the son of Omri did evil in the sight of the LORD **more than all who were before him.**
It came about, **as though it had been a trivial thing for him to walk in the sins of Jeroboam the son of Nebat, that he married Jezebel** the daughter of Ethbaal king of the Sidonians, and went to serve Baal and worshiped him. So he **erected an altar for Baal** in the house of Baal which he built in Samaria. Ahab also made the [a]**Asherah. Thus Ahab did more to provoke the LORD God of Israel than all the kings of Israel who were before him.**
Footnotes:

a. 1 Kings 16:33 I e wooden symbol of a female deity

In Matthew 23, Jesus is speaking to the earthly Jerusalem, where Ahab and Jezebel rule - the leaders of the wicked rebellious church that is still in operation even now.

Matthew 23:1-12 NASB

Then Jesus spoke to the crowds and to His disciples, saying: "The scribes and the Pharisees have **SEATED THEMSELVES** in the chair of Moses; therefore all that they tell you, do and observe, **BUT DO NOT DO ACCORDING TO THEIR DEEDS; FOR THEY SAY THINGS AND DO NOT DO THEM.** "They tie up heavy burdens and lay them on men's shoulders, but they themselves are **UNWILLING TO MOVE THEM WITH SO MUCH AS A FINGER...**

(Their worthless rhetoric about...

FOCUSING ON FAMILIES didn't manifest in my situation, as my wife openly tore our family apart - they could have simply told my wife to obey me, but they didn't. Why not? Jezebel can't obey Christ! She can only endorse the whoredom of Baal and Ashtoreth.)

Holy Whoredom

..."But they do all their deeds to **be noticed by men;** for they broaden their phylacteries and lengthen the tassels of their garments. "They **love the place of honor** at banquets and the **chief seats in the synagogues**, and **respectful greetings** in the market places, and being called Rabbi by men. "But do not be called Rabbi; for One is your Teacher, and you are all brothers. "Do not call anyone on earth your father; for One is your Father, He who is in heaven. "Do not be called leaders; for One is your Leader, that is, Christ. "But the greatest among you shall be your servant.

"Whoever exalts himself shall be humbled; and whoever humbles himself shall be exalted."

Eight Woes - Matthew 23:13-36

"But woe to **YOU** scribes and Pharisees, hypocrites, because **YOU** shut off the kingdom of heaven from people; for **YOU** do not enter in yourselves, **nor do YOU** allow those who are entering to go in.

["Woe to **YOU**, scribes and Pharisees, hypocrites, because **YOU** devour widows' houses, and **for a pretense you make long prayers;** therefore **YOU** will receive **greater condemnation.**]

"Woe to **YOU**, scribes and Pharisees, hypocrites, because **YOU** travel around on sea and land to make one proselyte; and when he becomes one, **YOU** make him **twice as much a son of hell as yourselves.**

"Woe to **YOU** blind guides, who say, 'Whoever swears by the temple, that is nothing; but whoever swears by the gold of the temple is obligated.'

"**YOU fools and blind men!** Which is more important, the gold or the temple that sanctified the gold?

"And, 'Whoever swears by the altar, that is nothing, but whoever swears by the offering on it, he is obligated.'

"**YOU** blind men, which is more important, the offering, or the altar that sanctifies the offering?

"Therefore, whoever swears by the altar, swears both by the altar and by everything on it.

"And whoever swears by the temple, swears both by the temple and by Him who dwells within it.

"And whoever swears by heaven, swears both by the throne of God and by Him who sits upon it.

"Woe to **YOU**, scribes and Pharisees, **hypocrites**!

For **YOU** tithe mint and dill and cummin, and have **neglected** the weightier provisions of the law:

<u>**JUSTICE** and **MERCY** and **FAITHFULNESS**</u>;

but these are the things **YOU** should have done without neglecting the others.

"**YOU** blind guides, <u>**who strain out a gnat and swallow a camel!**</u>

"Woe to **YOU** scribes and Pharisees, hypocrites!

For **YOU** clean the outside of the cup and of the dish, but inside they are full of robbery and **self-indulgence.**

"**YOU** blind Pharisee, first clean the inside of the cup and of the dish, so that the outside of it may become clean also.

"Woe to **YOU**, scribes and Pharisees, hypocrites! For **YOU** are like whitewashed tombs which on the outside appear beautiful, but inside they are full of dead men's bones and **all uncleanness.**

"So **YOU** too, outwardly **appear righteous to men,** but **inwardly YOU** are **full of hypocrisy and lawlessness.**

Holy Whoredom

"Woe to **YOU**, scribes and Pharisees, hypocrites! For **YOU** build the tombs of the prophets and adorn the monuments of the righteous, and say, 'If we had been living in the days of our fathers, we would not have been partners with them in shedding the blood of the prophets.'

"So **YOU** testify **against yourselves,** that **YOU** are sons of those who murdered the prophets.

"Fill up, then, the measure of the guilt of **YOUR** fathers.

"**YOU** serpents, **YOU** brood of vipers, **how** will **YOU** escape the **sentence of hell?**

"Therefore, behold, **I am sending YOU** <u>prophets and wise men and scribes</u>; some of them **YOU** will kill and crucify, and some of them **YOU** will scourge in your synagogues, and persecute from city to city, so that upon **YOU** may fall the guilt of all the righteous blood shed on earth, from the blood of righteous Abel to the blood of Zechariah, the son of Berechiah, whom **YOU** murdered between the temple and the altar.

"Truly I say to **YOU** all these things will come upon **THIS GENERATION."**

It is always "THIS GENERATION"

That which has been is that which will be...and that which has been done is that which will be done.

Believing that this reality was confined only to first century Palestine, is an absolute denial of Ecclesiastes 1. You have Jezebel making a reappearance as a spiritual principle in Revelation 2, about 900 years after her death. Yet, you refuse to accept the notion that everything Jesus said about the scribes and Pharisees has any validity now.

I love these depictions of Pharisees in christian films that make them out to look nefarious and openly prideful. That is not what they were like. Jesus said they looked outwardly righteous, probably appeared humble, and **PEOPLE REALLY LIKED THEM!!!** They were the Joel Osteens and Charles Stanleys of their day - totally respected and venerated by the masses of the church.

But that won't absolve them of the inevitable...

Chapter 8
Judgment, Recompense, and Vengeance

Ecclesiastes 11:9
"Rejoice, young man, during your childhood, and let your heart be pleasant during the days of young manhood. And **follow the impulses of your heart and the desires of your eyes, Yet know that God will bring you to judgment for all these things.**"

GO AHEAD AND FOOLISHLY GIVE YOURSELF OVER TO WHORING!
YOU'LL SEE WHAT HAPPENS!

Ecclesiastes 12:13-14 NASB
The conclusion, *WHEN ALL HAS BEEN HEARD*, is:
FEAR GOD
and keep His commandments,
because THIS APPLIES TO <u>EVERY</u> PERSON.

For... God **WILL** bring <u>EVERY</u> act to judgment,

<u>EVERYTHING</u> which is hidden,

whether it is good or evil.

Isaiah 34:7-9 NASB

Wild oxen will also fall with them
And young bulls with strong ones;
Thus their land will be **SOAKED WITH BLOOD,**
And their dust become greasy with fat.
For the LORD has a DAY OF VENGEANCE,
A YEAR OF RECOMPENSE for the cause of Zion.
Its streams will be turned into pitch,
And its loose earth into BRIMSTONE,
And its land will become BURNING PITCH.

Isaiah 47:2-4 NASB

Take the millstones and grind meal
Remove your veil, strip off the skirt,
Uncover the leg, cross the rivers.
"Your nakedness will be uncovered,
Your shame also will be exposed;
I will take vengeance and <u>will not spare a man</u>."
Our Redeemer, the LORD of hosts is His name,
The Holy One of Israel.

OK, are you going to retort something as insipid as:

"God forgives all my transgressions and casts them into the 'sea of forgetfulness'...He doesn't hold them against me anymore."

That is only true if He has been kind enough to lead you into godly sorrow producing genuine repentance, not the sorrow that the world (the earthly Jerusalem) produces.

BUT... IF YOUR GOSPEL ALLOWS YOU TO CONTINUE IN SIN, then there is no forgiveness.

I already quoted the first part of Hebrews chapter 6.

Holy Whoredom

Now read on...

Hebrews 6:1-8 NASB

Therefore **leaving the ELEMENTARY teaching about the Christ, <u>LET US PRESS ON TO MATURITY</u>,** not laying again a foundation of repentance from dead works and of faith toward God, of instruction about washings and laying on of hands, and the resurrection of the dead and eternal judgment. **AND THIS WE WILL DO, IF GOD PERMITS.**

<u>For in the case of those</u>

1. **who have once been enlightened**
2. and have tasted of the heavenly gift
3. and have been made partakers of the Holy Spirit,
4. and have tasted the good word of God
5. and the powers of the age to come,

and then have fallen away,

it is *impossible*

to renew them again to repentance,

since they again crucify to themselves the Son of God and put **Him to open shame.**

For *ground that drinks the rain* which often falls on it and brings forth vegetation useful to those for whose sake it is also tilled, receives a blessing from God; **BUT IF IT YIELDS THORNS AND THISTLES, IT IS WORTHLESS AND CLOSE TO BEING CURSED,**

<u>AND IT ENDS UP BEING BURNED.</u>

No one really understands what this is talking about, because it is found in the deep water of God's Word. It is buried far beneath the surface of mere naive understanding, that the uninformed and slow-witted kiddie pool preachers like **Bill Greenman, Bill Leveridge and Jason Haskell** misapply.

I am going to do you a favor here and let you repudiate once and for all, that you were ever born again while you continued in sin, adultery and idolatry, like the false gospel would have you believe that you can. According to the truth contained in the above verses, if you were, and fell away so radically, then it's game over - **YOU ARE DONE.** It would be advisable to abandon the silly unscriptural notion that you ever qualified for any of the five things listed above.

I have already shown you that sound doctrine is contained in the six tenets of the preceding verses, and you had been exposed to all kinds of confusing opinions as to the correct teachings on all of those subjects. So just acknowledge it, because if you want to stubbornly maintain that you have the Holy Spirit and have tasted the good Word of God while you are sinning, then there is nothing I can do to help you.

If you are humbled and my harsh words aren't finding their mark in you, then don't wear what I am saying to you. It is for those who are still prideful, but for some reason, can't put the book down.

I have been building on what I said before...

You are a...
thorn,
You are a...
briar,
You are...
an evil tree.

Worthless - **ONLY FIT FOR BURNING.** This is the judgment (A PRONOUNCMENT OF GUILT).

There is also recompense (repayment) for evil deeds, and vengeance. These three are closely related but not completely synonymous in scripture. There are different words for judgment - it would take too long to list all of them and their uses. I am trying to stick to the gospels and epistles for ease of understanding. I want you to look at one example in particular:

KRINO - STR. #2919 from Thayers
1. to judge
    a. to pronounce an opinion concerning right and wrong
        a. to be judged, i.e. summoned to trial that one's case may be examined and judgment passed upon it
    b. to pronounce judgment, **to subject to censure**
        a. of those who act the part of judges or arbiters in matters of common life, or pass judgment on the deeds and words of others
2. to rule, govern
    a. to preside over with the power of giving judicial decisions, because it was the prerogative of kings and rulers to pass judgment
3. to contend together, of warriors and combatants
    a. to dispute
    b. in a forensic sense
        a. to go to law, have suit at law

(This is a legal, judicial word at it's core, and is most commonly translated as judge.)

Matthew 7:1-2 NASB
"Do not judge **(krino - unrighteously)** so that you will not be judged **(krino - righteously)**. "For IN THE WAY you judge, **(krino - righteously OR unrighteously)** you will be judged; **(krino - righteously)** and by your standard of measure, it will be measured to you." **(only much more severely multiplied).**

Here is the text that *explains* what Jesus was actually talking about, THE WAY IN WHICH YOU JUDGE:

1 Corinthians 6:1-9 NASB
Lawsuits *Discouraged*
(ANOTHER LIE - Discouraged?
Try "condemned".)
Does any one of you, when he has a case against his neighbor,

DARE to **GO TO LAW** (krino - unrighteously)

before the unrighteous and not before the saints?

Or do you not know that the saints

will judge **(krino - righteously)** the world?

If the world is judged by you,

are you not competent to constitute the smallest law courts?

Do you not know that we will judge **(krino - righteously)** angels?

How much more matters of this life?

So if you have law courts dealing with matters of this life,

do you appoint them as judges who are of no account in the church?

I say this to your shame, I say this to your shame, I say this to your shame, I say this to your shame, I say this to YOUR SHAME...

Is it so, that **there is not among you**

one wise man who will be able to decide...

*(#1252 **diakrino - righteously -** to learn by discrimination, to try, decide, to determine, give judgment, decide a dispute)*

...between his brethren, **(apparently not!)**

but brother **goes to law** (krino - unrighteously)
with brother, and that **before unbelievers**?

Actually, then, **it is already a defeat (failure) for you,** that you have lawsuits with one another.

Why not rather be wronged?

(Because I deserve the happiness God wants for me...)

Why not rather be defrauded?

(Because suffering and laying down is for suckers...)

On the contrary,

YOU YOURSELVES WRONG AND DEFRAUD.

You do this EVEN TO YOUR BRETHREN.

Or **DO YOU NOT KNOW** that the

unrighteous will not inherit the kingdom of God?

(This disinheritance is the direct result of the unrighteous use of civil courts CONDEMNED IN THIS PASSAGE!)

Do not be deceived...
Do not be deceived...
Do not be deceived...

Now there are two kinds of judgment going on here - unrighteous - earthly judgment that you will, in rebellion, seek from the same godless court system that promotes the wholesale slaughter of unborn children. Then, there is the impending JUDGMENT OF GOD that is being stored up (pressed down, compacted, condensed), and will be measured back to those who dismiss the clear command to NOT take ANYONE to unrighteous courts.

This would include divorce! I told this to my wife, that it was sinful for her to defraud me. Why were all the christians who knew us, so ignorant of this clear prohibition? Because it says "discouraged" in the heading, implying, **"Well, it isn't God's best course of action to take, but if you have been wronged, then go on and take him to the cleaners and be happy."**

Well, she did - I have nothing now and I am still being oppressed daily, based on lies and false testimony. I have child support still being accrued to me for my son who is now twenty years old, since I never filed a single paper to the godless court system - **because I am willing to obey:**

1 Corinthians 6:7b NASB

Why not rather be wronged?
Why not rather be defrauded?

Remember, none of this is comprehensive, so don't get indignant and say, **"You are leaving out important stuff about this word's use."** I know I am leaving out volumes of information, but I can't go into depth on every mention of this word in the Bible - well over 100 times in 99 verses. Then there is its noun form #2920 - judgment. In order to discern or judge sound doctrine rightly, you have to know all of the places where this is mentioned and the words that surround them in other verses. It is very complex. This is not that kind of book.

None of this can be explained in any significant detail, because I cannot write the way in which I think. When I see any verse, my mind instantly goes into **concordance mode,** then categorizes and compares words and verses where those words appear. It is the putting together of words with the phrases (thoughts) where they are combined in scripture.

1 Corinthians 2:12-14 NASB

Now **we** have received, *not the spirit of the world*, **but the Spirit who is from God,**

SO THAT **we** may know the things freely given to us by God,

which things **we** also speak, not in words taught by human wisdom, **but in those taught by the Spirit,** <u>combining spiritual thoughts with spiritual words</u>.

But a natural man, a natural man...

...a natural man,
does not accept the things of the Spirit of God,
for they are FOOLISHNESS TO HIM;
and he cannot understand them,
because they are spiritually appraised.

This is the scriptural explanation of how revelation works, as I detailed it on page 126 in the previous chapter. I wish I had the time to run down all of the verses where krino and #2920 "krisis" appear. Hmm...sounds a lot like crisis, doesn't it? That will be one for you to look into for yourself!

But there will be a TIME...

1 Corinthians 4:5 NASB
Therefore do not go on **passing judgment**
(krino - unrighteously) before THE TIME,
but wait until the Lord comes
who will both bring to light the things hidden in the darkness
and **disclose the motives of men's hearts;**
and then each man's praise will come to him from God.

So much for the brief lesson on judgment. There is a type of judgment we are to exercise before the time, which is an assessing or evaluating of something's merit, in terms of its righteousness. It is not the same as issuing a sentence of condemnation, or oppressing one's neighbor by the use of unrighteous courts. It is judging (krino) evil, unrighteous, sinful behavior, without the punitive and oppressive consequences of earthly courts (which Jesus said the wicked would drag you before, if you were His disciple).

The same word, "krino", is found in chapter 5 immediately preceding 1 Corinthians 6, where the proper righteous use of judging is contrasted with it's unrighteous misuse in chapter 6. This is a rebuke that should be included with chapter 6 because it is the same subject - **the lying pen of the scribes again destroying the continuity by inserting a division...**

...For what have I to do with judging **(krino - righteously)** outsiders?

Do you not judge (krino - unrighteously) those who are within the church?

...But those who are outside, God judges **(krino - righteously)**.

REMOVE THE WICKED MAN FROM AMONG YOURSELVES.

He is saying that you take your brothers to unrighteous civil courts, but you don't have the sense or the stones (balls) to kick someone to the curb, who is sexually immoral **(committing adultery with an elder's wife)**, so that God can judge them!

See, this is what should be done in churches all over America, calling adulterers to repent (leave) their sinful unions - **YEAH!** like that is going to happen. But hey, slavery finally ended in America, and that was supported and scripturally justified in the whore church too, so who knows?

If they don't repent, Jesus tells you what you are to do.

Matthew 18:15-17 NASB

"If your brother sins, go and show him his fault in private; if he listens to you, you have won your brother.

"But if he does not listen to you, take one or two more with you, so that BY THE MOUTH OF TWO OR THREE WITNESSES EVERY FACT MAY BE CONFIRMED.

"If he refuses to listen to them, tell it to the church; <u>and if he refuses to listen even to the church, let him be to you as a Gentile and a tax collector."</u>

Who gets kicked out of church nowadays? But you wanna **play church** and this is one of the only two times the word "ekklesia" (church) is mentioned in the gospels. You have a prime directive from Jesus of how the operation of the church is to be carried out, and it is wholly ignored - **UNBELIEVABLE!**

I followed this very procedure with my wife, and christian ministers and pastors completely ignored it. Both of these idiot christian ministers (and I use that term loosely) told me the exact same insipid thing, *"Divorce isn't God's best."*

Let them bear their SHAME for strengthening my wife's evil hands:

- Purpose International: **Bill Greenman** - False Prophet, **Balaam's Error (http://www.purpose3.com/)**
- New Creation Church: **Craig Colorado** - Chief priest of Baal Jason Haskell and High priestess of Ashtoreth: Tracey Haskell, **Synagogue of Satan in Craig, CO (http://ncccraig.com/)**
- Then we have Jay Ruben Guerra - an entirely different classification of insensitive christian douchebag. I spoke with him recently and he stubbornly maintains my wife should not reconcile with me. I used to call Bill and Jay my friends, but now they are callously indifferent to my plight. The Lord will recompense them according to their deeds. You can find him on Facebook (he lives in the Raymore, MO) if you want to reprove him for his sinful wickedness.

There were others who at least deserve a mention who either didn't say anything or actively assisted my wife in her rebellion:

- Merril Upchurch - an adulterer himself who is married to a woman who is NOT lawfully his, but he thinks he is pleasing the Lord. Even though he and I would have conversations about the Bible, I had no idea how unclean and vile he was. He would say with smug satisfaction that sodomites were reprobates, but he was blind to his own whoring depravity with his harlot wife Linda.
- Pam Williams - another vile, whoring, remarried Jezebel, came to support Mary at our initial divorce hearing, I think just to glare at me. She is in for the surprise of her life when she is brought before God, to answer for her deplorable actions concerning my marriage.

Then, I recently followed this same procedure with a wronged woman, whose covenant husband divorced her and married a woman who also had divorced her covenant husband.

We went to her husband's and his whore's vile pastor to ask for assistance in reproving him. And you guessed it - coward that he was, he refused to do anything, because they are a pagan sex temple of Baal and Ashtoreth.

- Sulphur (*brimstone*) baptist church in Sulphur, OK. Reprobate pastor and head **GIVER of hearty approval** - Bill Leveridge, Jezebel's Sex Temple **(www.sulphurfbc.org)**

No one does what the Lord commands, yet they think that they love Him, even though He stated matter-of-factly:

"If you love me, you will keep my commandments."

Matthew 7:21-23 NASB
"Not everyone who says to Me, 'Lord, Lord,' will enter the kingdom of heaven,

but he who does the will of My Father who is in heaven will enter.

"Many will say to Me on that day, 'Lord, Lord, did we not prophesy in Your name, and in Your name cast out demons,

and in Your name perform many miracles?'

"AND THEN I WILL DECLARE TO THEM,
'I never never never never never never knew you;
DEPART FROM ME, YOU WHO PRACTICE LAWLESSNESS.'"

What is practicing lawlessness? Is that really a tough question?

Anything that is disobedient to Christ's commandments is LAWLESSNESS. Do you really believe that you can have unrighteous earthly lawsuits with the spouse whom you promised to love, honor, and obey, and be submitting to the law of Christ? This is how rebellious the whole house of Israel is, completely ignoring the plain prohibition of 1 Corinthians 6 to not take anyone to court, much less a BROTHER.

You know I started with judgment, but I think I need to back down the staircase one level to the ground floor, where everyone is standing, pointing their fingers in everyone else's face, unrighteously. It is the sad condition of the entire human race. I want you to look at these concepts as steps on a staircase - judgment being the first step up from the ground (earth), where those who are carnal dwell.

John 3:36 NASB
He who believes in the Son **HAS HAS HAS HAS** eternal life; but he who **DOES NOT OBEY THE SON** will not see life, but the **WRATH OF GOD ABIDES ON HIM.**

I want you to notice something very profound here. This statement is emphatic. There is only one thing required for someone to have God's wrath (burning white hot anger) abiding on them. I don't have time to detail this term's use in scripture - again, do your own research. But this is not some action that is seen in the natural, it is His anger that isn't sensual or visible. All that is required according to this verse is to be disobeying the Son. How much disobedience would that entail? You don't have to do much to have God angry with you. Just disobey one thing and it is rebellion - but the false gospel of licentious grace will keep you in sin until the day of your death. That is antithetical to the **TRUTH OF THE GOSPEL.**

If these words are not sinking in, then you missed a boatload of points I have already made. You need to go back and reread the beginning of this book. Paul said that empty ritual (circumcision, singing songs, water baptism, communion...) is meaningless... What counts is keeping the commandments of God.

Ten commandments?
More like 10,000!

Hosea 8:11-13 NASB

Since Ephraim has multiplied altars for sin, **They have become altars of sinning for him.** Though I wrote for him

TEN THOUSAND PRECEPTS OF MY LAW, THEY ARE REGARDED...AS A STRANGE THING.

As for My sacrificial gifts, They sacrifice the flesh and eat it, **But the LORD has taken no delight in them.** Now He will remember their iniquity, and punish them for their sins; They will return to Egypt.

Everything above needs to be highlighted, because it all applies in regard to the whore church, that multitudes of christians attend every Sunday. **Multiplied altars of sinning, that the Lord takes zero delight in.** But you won't believe that will you? Do you think that this concept has no basis in your **"New Testament"?** Well, lookey here!

Matthew 18:23-25 NASB

"For this reason the kingdom of heaven may be compared to a king who wished to settle accounts with his slaves.

"When he had begun to settle them, one who owed him **TEN THOUSAND** talents was brought to him.

"But since he did not have the means to repay, his lord commanded him to be sold, along with his wife and children and all that he had, and repayment to be made."

If you track all of these key words down, those ten thousand talents are the silver commands of God's Word, and every slave is guilty of all.

James 2:10 NASB

For whoever keeps the whole law and yet stumbles *in one point*, **he has become guilty of all.**

There are "do this" and "don't do that" commands. I have never taken the time to personally count them all, but there probably are 10,000. I don't believe it is a metaphor.

I wrote Jay Guerra an email and gave him 1 Thessalonians 5:20-22 and told him he was disobeying four commandments (19-22 below). Did he listen? No. He couldn't obey Christ, not even in those four commandments, **but** he claims that he is in Christ. That is nonsense.

God's Word says to examine or prove everything. Christians do not want to investigate anything, they want to be spoon fed the poison Pablum that their iniquitous shepherd regurgitates week in and week out.

How many commands of Christ are in this one short passage?

1 Thessalonians 5:11-27 NASB

1. Therefore **encourage** one another
2. And **build up** one another, just as you also are doing
3. We request of you, brethren, that you **appreciate those who** diligently labor among you
4. **AND** *(that you appreciate those who)* have charge over you in the Lord
5. **AND** *(that you appreciate those who)* give you instruction,
6. And that you **esteem** them very highly in love because of their work
7. **Live** in peace with one another
8. We urge you, brethren, **admonish** the unruly *(Warn the insubordinate/rebellious)*,
9. **Encourage** the fainthearted
10. **Help** the weak (Would this not apply to anyone who is being divorced - dragged to court by a rebellious spouse?)
11. **Be** patient with everyone
12. **See that** no one repays another with evil for evil (Isn't divorce hated by God?...making it an evil act?)
13. but always **seek after** that which is good for one another
14. and *(Always seek after that which is good)* for all people
15. **Rejoice** always
16. **Pray** without ceasing
17. In everything **give** thanks

18. **Do not quench** the Spirit
19. **Do not despise** prophetic utterances
20. But **examine** everything carefully
21. **Hold fast** to that which is good
22. **Abstain** from every form of evil (Any need to elaborate?)
23. Brethren, **pray** for us
24. **Greet** all the brethren with a holy kiss
25. I adjure you by the Lord to **have this letter read** to all the brethren

There are twenty-five commandments just listed here **(verbs - do this or don't do that)** that are a **strange thing** to most christians, because their **altars are only made for sinning,** not for obeying the commands of Christ, which Paul said:

1 Corinthians 14:37 NASB
If anyone thinks he is a prophet or spiritual, **let him recognize** that the things which I write to you are the Lord's **commandment**.

I will make the same bold assertion without any fear of speaking idly - I am writing **The Lord's commandment** as well. This is a chapter about what? Judgment - but there must of necessity be something to judge.

Disobedience that incurs God's wrath is in need of judging in the earthly church that hates Christ, because they flippantly disregard and trivialize His edicts. So, everyone is standing on the ground floor of God's burning hot wrath and can't FEEL a thing? How could people not be cognizant of God's wrath?

It is only revealed from heaven where the righteous dwell.

Romans 1:18
For the **wrath** of God is revealed <u>**from heaven**</u> against all ungodliness and unrighteousness of men who suppress the truth in unrighteousness.

Romans 2:5
But because of your stubbornness and unrepentant heart <u>you are storing up **wrath** for yourself</u> in the day of **wrath** and revelation of the righteous judgment of God...

Holy Whoredom

Everyone is under God's wrath, which is as unseen as the adultery that remarried people are committing. The passage on wrath in **Romans 1 designates covenant-breakers as being under God's wrath, as much as those who practice sodomy and lesbianism**. You need to quit pointing your bony index finger at the faggots and bulldykes, and recognize where your other three fingers are pointing!

As long as you continue in disobedience to any and all of The Son's commands, you are continuing to store up wrath to your account. Nothing else will dissipate God's displeasure with you. Do you think that a meaningless assent to Christ's Lordship automatically delivers you from God's indignation?

Go on believing that nonsense, and see how far it gets you on judgment day!

Matthew 12:36 NASB
But I tell you that <u>**every careless word that people speak**</u>, they shall give an accounting for it in the day of judgment.

If you are still speaking careless (idle) words, it is only evidence that God has not yet brought you to judgment and **delivered you from His wrath.**

Romans 5:9 NASB
Much more then, having now been justified by His blood, we shall be saved from the **wrath** of God through Him.

If you are still doing things that evidence God's wrath upon you (disobeying), then you are not "saved" or "justified" according to the plain teaching of scripture. So, quit speaking idly by insisting that you are - this is only bringing more wrath upon you that will require…

RECOMPENSE

Isaiah 61:8 NASB
For I, the LORD, love justice, I hate robbery in the burnt offering; And **I will faithfully give them their RECOMPENSE…** And make an everlasting covenant with them.

Romans 2:5-9 NASB

But because of your stubbornness and unrepentant heart you are **storing up wrath for yourself in the day of wrath and revelation of the righteous judgment of God,** who **will render to each person according to his deeds:** to those who by perseverance in doing good seek for glory and honor and immortality, eternal life; but to those who are selfishly ambitious and do not obey the truth, but obey unrighteousness, wrath and indignation. **There will be tribulation and distress for every soul of man who does evil,** of the Jew first and also of the Greek, but glory and honor and peace to everyone who does good, to the Jew first and also to the Greek...

Nobody is off of the hook for these verses. Everyone will be judged with equity, because everyone is an evil tree. A baby who dies is not going to be recompensed as severely as your wicked pastor, who ignored Christ's commands to not be complicit in the marriage of two adulterers. He should know better, **but he is blinded by his greed and cowardice.** The amount of recompense or rendering is according to your deeds. There isn't anyone who escapes God's righteous judgment, but the longer you continue sinning and offending others and God by your rebellious acts and speech, the more God is required to repay you. **This is detailed here:**

2 Corinthians 5:10 NASB

For we must all appear before the **judgment** seat of Christ, so that each one may be **recompensed** for his deeds in the body, according to what he has done, **whether good or bad.**

Let me ask you a question, maybe you can explain this to me. So, we christians die and go to heaven, according to the mythological gospel. Then, at some point in the future, God rounds us up and repays us for our evil deeds, after we have spent hundreds or possibly thousands of years in heaven waiting for Christ to tell us to saddle up on our white horses so we can ride back to earth with Him?

I could never understand that verse in 2 Corinthians 5, until He delivered me from the confusion of the evil Babylonian whore's poisonous elixir, that I all too willingly drank. All of God's servants must drink it. The hard thing is to stop. I am going to get you sobered up, if you will LISTEN.

I have appeared before the judgment seat already. He has judged me, cut down my worthless wicked tree, and planted a new good tree that can only produce good, righteous, holy, fruit. It may only look like a mean, cantankerous, and hateful tree to you, because it doesn't appeal to the WHORING woman in the garden either - she falls for the serpent's lies every time. There is nothing attractive about the tree of life.

I can assure you that I hate you no more than Christ hated the Pharisees. This harsh reproof is so that you may be **sound** (healthy/whole - *like sound doctrine*) in the faith. You are deeply and desperately sick. So we have stepped up from the ground onto righteous judgment, then we stepped up again to recompense.

NOW, THE TOP STEP IS...
VENGEANCE - BLOOD SOAKED AND ABLAZE WITH FLAMING FIRE

Isaiah 35:4 NASB
Say to those with **anxious heart,**

"Take courage, fear not Behold,

your **God will come with <u>vengeance</u>;**

The **<u>recompense</u> of God will come**...

But He will save you."

There are different people being referenced here. There are the anxious of heart, the elect. There is vengeance to be meted out by God on behalf of the elect. There are those to be recompensed for evil deeds - the wicked who oppress the righteous. This is summed up quite nicely in this parable that people think is only about persevering in prayer.

Believer X

Luke 18:1-8 NASB
Now He was telling them a parable to show that at all times they ought to pray and not to lose heart, saying,"In a certain city there was a judge (#2923 from root - krino) who did not fear God and did not respect man. "There was a widow in that city, and she kept coming to him, saying, 'Give me legal protection from my opponent.' **"For a while he was unwilling;** but afterward he said to himself, 'Even though I do not fear God nor respect man, yet **because this widow bothers me, I will give her legal protection,** otherwise by continually coming she will wear me out.'"

And the Lord said, "Hear what the **unrighteous judge** said; NOW (there is whole bunch of stuff that must be inserted into this gap in order to apply what comes next), will not God bring about JUSTICE (Ekdikesis) for **HIS ELECT** who cry to Him day and night, and will He delay long over them? "I tell you that He will bring about JUSTICE **(VENGEANCE)** for them quickly. However, when the Son of Man comes, will He find faith on the earth?"

Why are the elect crying out day and night? What are they seeking?

THEY ARE AWAITING GOD'S PROMISED VENGEANCE!

Ekdikesis - from Thayers

1. **a revenging, VENGEANCE, punishment** (In 2 Cor 7:11 -- meeting out of justice; doing justice to all parties. See Luke 18:3, 21:22. The word also has the sense of acquittal and **carries the sense of vindication**. - Vincent III p. 329)

What you are missing is - this widow is the evil whore going before an unrighteous judge - dragging the Elect of God to the

153

unrighteous judges of the world, just like the Jews dragged Jesus before Pilate. You must die in the same manner in which He died. Look at the detail. They brought Jesus before Pilate two times. The first time that they brought Jesus, Pilate was unwilling, then he changed his mind.

You must suffer injustice at the hands of the wicked, or you are NOT THE ELECT (chosen) of God! So again, I will warn you to quit claiming things for yourself that you have no business claiming. I am God's elect. You may not like it, but it is true.

Psalm 13 NASB
How long shall I take counsel in my soul,
Having sorrow in my heart all the day?
How long will my enemy be exalted over me?

Revelation 6:9-11 NASB
When the Lamb broke the fifth seal, I saw underneath the altar the souls of those who had **been slain because of the word of God, and because of the testimony which they had maintained;** and they cried out with a loud voice, saying,

"How long, O Lord, **holy and true, will You refrain from judging and avenging our blood on those who dwell on the earth?"**
And there was given to each of them a **white robe; and they were told that they should rest for a little while longer,** until the number of their fellow servants and their brethren who were to be killed even as they had been, would be completed also.

I have my white robe. I have already died and, having maintained my testimony, now I cry out awaiting the vengeance that is promised me. He will bring about the blood-soaked vengeance in flaming fire. If you do not suffer, you do not inherit God's kingdom. Do not go on deceiving yourself with empty words.

If you have nothing for God to avenge you of, then He didn't choose you...

2 Thessalonians 1:4-8 NASB

Therefore, we ourselves speak proudly of you among the churches of God for **your perseverance and faith in the midst of all your persecutions and afflictions which you endure.** This is a **plain indication** of God's righteous judgment **so that you will be considered worthy of the kingdom of God, for which indeed you are suffering.** For after all it is only just for God to repay with affliction those who afflict you, and to give **relief to you who are afflicted** and to us as well when the Lord Jesus will be revealed from heaven with His mighty angels in flaming fire, dealing out **retribution to those who do not know God and to those <u>who do not obey the gospel of our Lord Jesus</u>.**

Do **you believe** Jesus' words concerning marriage, divorce, and remarriage, that I have clearly outlined to you in this book, are **not** the gospel also?

...These will **pay the penalty of eternal destruction, away from the presence of the Lord** and from the glory of His power...

I do complain (that isn't sinful - it is part of fulfilling scripture) because it is hard, but I do not nullify its purpose in my life. It has refined me to speak God's Word. I am His oracle. I thought it would be much less difficult, like all do. Salvation isn't easy or without hardship.

You will endure the same, if you walk away from the whore - your friends will think that you have **"gone off of the deep end"** or **"are in need of psychological treatment to restore your mental health"** or that **"you must be crazy!"** Well, Jesus' family wanted to have him committed too, so I am in good company.

Jesus told His generation that there would be vengeance upon the literal city of Jerusalem, because of the way in which He knew that they would treat Him. Sure enough, the vengeance did come in 70 A.D. when Titus' army razed the city that turned over the Son of God to the Romans to be scourged and crucified.

So again, here is the order:

> **THIS TOP STEP IS RESERVED
> EXCLUSIVELY FOR THE ELECT**
>
> # VENGEANCE
> ## RECOMPENSE
> ### JUDGMENT
> #### WRATH

Everyone is born under God's wrath - a non-negotiable reality. One step up is God's righteous judgment, which no one will escape, even though it may sometimes appear that way.

1 Timothy 5:24-25 NASB
The sins of some men are quite evident, going before them to judgment; **for others, their sins follow after.** Likewise also, deeds that are good are quite evident, and those which are otherwise **(sinful) cannot be concealed (FOREVER).**

If you do not get what this is saying, it is this: whether open rebellion or things done in secret, **EVERYTHING will ALL one day be brought to light.** Grace that you claim does not hide the inevitable certainty of this being fulfilled in you.

Isaiah 47:2 NASB
Remove your veil, strip off the skirt, Uncover the leg,
"Your nakedness _will be_ uncovered,
Your shame also _will be_ exposed."

Don't believe those liars of the circumcision who will tell you that your sins are continually being washed away with the precious blood of Jesus. That is outright blasphemy. They will condone and foster rebellion in their ranks because, like Ted Haggard, a sodomite, yet **president** of the National Association of Evangelicals (NAE) from 2003 until November 2006, they are slaves of corruption.

2 Peter 2:18-19 NASB

For speaking out **arrogant words of vanity** they entice by fleshly desires, by sensuality, those who barely escape from the ones who live in error, promising them freedom while they

THEMSELVES ARE SLAVES OF CORRUPTION;

for by what a man is overcome, by this he is enslaved.

Most of these false prophets are nicely adorned tombs, but inside they are unclean in every way. These are Jesus' words and the few who have been exposed by the secular media will pale in comparison when God wakes them up from the dust of the earth and begins to **uncover all of their blasphemous misdeeds, which they have committed in His name.**

So then, to summarize:

Everyone is under God's **wrath**, everyone will be **judged**, everyone will be **recompensed** (repayed) for their good or evil deeds, but ONLY the elect will be **avenged** by God. He is under no obligation to avenge the wicked of the wrongs committed against them. If you seek earthly justice, you will negate any retribution that God would do for you.

Chapter 9
Sordid Gain

2 Peter 2:3-15

"AND IN THEIR GREED THEY WILL EXPLOIT YOU WITH FALSE WORDS..."

But these, like **unreasoning animals,** born as creatures of instinct to be captured and killed, **reviling where they have no knowledge**, will in the destruction of those creatures also be destroyed, suffering wrong as the wages of doing wrong.
They count it a pleasure to revel in the daytime. They are **stains and blemishes**, reveling in their deceptions, as they carouse with you, having **eyes full of adultery** that **never cease from sin,** enticing unstable souls, **having a heart trained in greed,** accursed children; forsaking the right way, they have gone astray, having followed the way of Balaam, the son of Beor, who loved the **wages of unrighteousness....**

I have had run-ins with more than my share of these dumb animals. They will not humble themselves to the word of Christ that flows out of me like clean cold water. They just start in by impugning my character and literally misquoting my very words. They have a record of my words on the website which they could easily copy and paste - but instead, they attribute things to me which I never said. It only confirms my position, it doesn't even bother me anymore. It did initially, but when I realized this is a mark of God's approval, I am only pleased by it and laugh when it happens now.

Believer X

My last communique with Jezebel (Cathy) the other night had me howling with laughter. She called me Satan and actually admitted that I uncovered the bones in her white-washed tomb. What she doesn't know, is that she is heaping up more wrath and judgment to herself that will be repayed (pressed down, shaken together, and running over) one solemn day.

But, even though they should tremble, the scripture says that they are unable. There are dozens, if not hundreds of verses, dealing with greed and coveting what isn't yours.

I do not do this for money, it does me no good right now anyway. Because of my whore wife's oppressive use of the court system, I cannot even have a checking account or a credit or debit card. The profits from my business have been stolen from me by my whoring christian sister. The proceeds from the court-enforced sale of my house have been unrighteously "borrowed" and wasted by my now dead father. I have no means with which to conduct business in any practical manner in this world.

I do not covet your money. The main reason this book is being sold is so that it can be distributed more widely. I offered the gospel freely, but no one wanted it. My goal is not to make money - I don't believe that I will. My goal is to bring about change, however small, and encourage those who want the truth.

1 Peter 5:1-3 NASB
Therefore, I exhort the elders among you,
as your fellow elder and witness of the sufferings of Christ,
and a partaker also of the glory that is to be revealed,
shepherd (pastor) the flock of God among you,
exercising oversight not under compulsion,
but voluntarily, according to the will of God;

and NOT for SORDID GAIN,

but with eagerness;
nor yet as lording it over those allotted to your charge,
but proving to be examples to the flock.

Does it ever bother anyone that pastors of all these MEGA-churches draw enormous salaries and get lucrative book deals in order to preach and promote things that contradict **sound doctrine**? I mean really step back and look at things objectively for one moment. What is so orthodox about orthodoxy? The plethora of books on every subject in christian bookstores with so many differing views doesn't even give you pause?

I mentioned this earlier. Truth is like math, certain and immutable. There is no way you would tolerate your children's math textbook having multiple solutions for the same equation. Well, math expert A says $2+2 = 5$, and math expert B says $2+2 = 3.5$, and math expert C says $2+2 = y$. That is just silliness, but you abide all of the false teaching **IN THE CHURCH** and call it merely **"a difference of opinion"**.

Tell me, where do you find this kind of nonsense in scripture? Legitimate apostles being confused over correct doctrine?

You can point to the council at Jerusalem in Acts 15, but they were still carnal when those rules were handed down, because when Paul wrote 1 Corinthians, he said eating things sacrificed to idols was neither here nor there - it made no difference in regards to true faith (1 Corinthians chapters 8 and 10).

The proponents of apostolic faith, when the **SPIRIT OF TRUTH** is given (*not in Acts 2*, when the initial outpouring occurred, but later), are never in disagreement over **anything.** This essential/non-essential hogwash is just a ruse to keep you entangled in the whore church's web of deceit. This whole machine needs your money to pay for their extravagant facilities and lifestyles of the rich and infamous.

Let's look at the SHAMELESS LIE of the tithe:

This is going to offend many because their pastors will not tell you what the tithe is and its real purpose in the OLD COVENANT which they are binding themselves to.

Leviticus 27:30 NASB
Thus all the **tithe of the land**, of the **seed of the land** or of the **fruit of the tree**, is the LORD'S; it is holy to the LORD.

Numbers 18:24 NASB

"For the **tithe** of the sons of Israel, which they offer as an offering to the LORD, I have given to the **Levites for an inheritance**; therefore I have said concerning them, ' **They shall have no inheritance *(OF LAND)* among the sons of Israel.'"**

Let me break this down in a nutshell. This is absolutely true. The tithe was for the tribe of Levi who performed the temple service. They were given no allotment of land in which to raise livestock and produce. They could not be self sustaining in an agriculturally based society. So the Lord provided them a means to feed themselves.

The tenth of all the livestock (that is, the **tenth to pass under the rod** - not the first - meaning, if you only had nine cows, then you didn't tithe any), that the other tribes produced and a tenth of all the fruit and seed crops were to be given to the **LEVITICAL PRIESTHOOD.** Money was never tithed in scripture - the only time money was connected to tithing was here:

Deuteronomy 14:22-29 NASB

"You shall surely tithe all the produce from what you sow, which comes out of the field every year.
"<u>You</u> **shall eat in the presence of the LORD your God,** at the place where He chooses to establish His name, **the tithe of your grain, your new wine, your oil, and the firstborn of your herd and your flock,** so that you may learn to fear the LORD your God always."

Now watch this:

"**If the distance is so great for you that you are not able to bring the tithe**, since the place where the LORD your God chooses to set His name is too far away from you when the LORD your God blesses you, then **you shall exchange it for money,** and bind the money in your hand and go to the place which the LORD your God chooses.

"**You may spend the money for whatever your heart desires**: for oxen, or sheep, or wine, **or strong drink, or whatever your heart desires; and there you shall eat in the presence of the LORD your God and rejoice, you and your household.** "

Holy Whoredom

Also you shall not **neglect the Levite who is in your town, for he has no portion or inheritance among you.** "At the end of every third year you shall bring out all the tithe of your produce in that year, and shall deposit it in your town. "The Levite, because he has no portion or inheritance among you, and the alien, the orphan and the widow who are in your town, shall come and eat and be satisfied, in order that the LORD your God may bless you in all the work of your hand which you do."

Where are all these tithing parties? They sound like a blast!!! But NOOO...your money grubbing pastor won't tell you about **THIS TITHE**, since that would cut into his profit margins! In case you missed it, they HAD money, but it was never to be tithed. This is a clever misapplication of scripture (that we use money and they didn't). They had money in verses 25-26, **to spend on whatever their (THE PEOPLE'S) hearts desired!**

If pastors really want to play this tithing game then here is how it needs to go down according to scripture:

They give up their personal real estate holdings, live on the church premises, and collect livestock and produce. Then they use it to feed themselves and their family and for burnt offerings, grain offerings, thank offerings, etc...since they want to impose old covenant traditions and rules upon you.

Then, let them tell you that they (the liars who collect tithes) are the **ONLY PRIESTHOOD**, and you are no longer a kingdom of priests, like it says here:

Revelation 1:5-6 NASB

Jesus Christ, the faithful witness, the firstborn of the dead, and the ruler of the kings of the earth To Him who loves us and released us from our sins by His blood--and He has **made us to be a kingdom, priests** to His God and Father--to Him be the glory and the dominion forever and ever. Amen.

This is beginning to sound to me a lot like **sordid gain** AND **hearts trained in greed** AND **wages of unrighteousness.** But hey, what do I know? I didn't attend seminary and have not a letter after my name, other than X.

You poor stupid sheep need to read your Bibles from cover to cover, several times like I did as a young christian, so that you can see through the **HYPOCRISY** and duplicitous manipulations that these wicked men will use to enslave you.

If you can't see that the tithe is a convenient tradition **they are putting you in bondage to**, then what else can I say? But that is not their only transgression in this area of greed. They use the proclamation of the false gospel as a means to bilk unsuspecting fools into wasting their heirs' money on a lie.

Matthew 23:14 NASB

"Woe to you, scribes and Pharisees, hypocrites,
**because you devour widows' houses,
and for a pretense you make long prayers;**
therefore you will receive **greater condemnation."**

2 Timothy 3:5-7 NASB

Holding to a form of godliness,
although they have denied its power;
Avoid such men as these.
For among them are **those who enter into households
and *captivate* weak women weighed down with sins,
led on by various impulses,
ALWAYS LEARNING AND NEVER ABLE
TO COME TO THE KNOWLEDGE OF THE TRUTH.**

I can't tell you how much money my poor deceived grandmother wasted on Billy Graham, and her baptist church's missions and building funds, but I'd be willing to bet it was a small fortune. The sad reality, is that it will not earn her any lasting reward from God. Poor manipulated older women are taken in by these hustlers and left with nothing, because they believe that they are giving into God's work and the furthering of the gospel of the Lord Jesus.

I have already proven that these men do not have sound doctrine, which is **THE FOUNDATION**, therefore they do not have the Father, nor the Son. If you missed it, go back and read the chapter on sound doctrine again.

So, these lying ministers peddle their useless books and seminars to keep you chasing the proverbial carrot on a stick by promising you all kinds of **happiness, wealth, and spiritual fulfillment.**

But it never really actually manifests in the overwhelming majority of people who follow these harebrained formulas. I am aware that they have their shining testimonials, but that is like the disclaimer at the bottom of every infomercial - *"results not typical, your results may vary."* I will give you odds of about 1,000 to 1, that your results will vary greatly from the handful of people who boast success with any program.

The truth of the gospel is 100% certain. If you lose your life, you will find it, **but you must lose it.** It is not some meaningless ritual of a prayer, a splash, and a tenth of your hard-earned paycheck (before taxes I might add).

AND IN THEIR GREED THEY WILL EXPLOIT YOU WITH FALSE WORDS...

There is no way for you to avoid this - THE SCRIPTURE CANNOT BE BROKEN. You have been exploited - it is a needful part of the process. It is regrettable, but you must acknowledge the word **"WILL"** here. It doesn't say *"might"* **EXPLOIT YOU** - it says **"WILL,"** just like **Jezebel WILL lead you astray**. If you are truly His bond-servant, you are to be exploited in your ignorance, by these liars of the circumcision. I was, until I woke up and found myself in bed with Leah! God had tricked me! I did not have the presence of mind to **"check under the hood"** and decided to get drunk on my wedding night. Then I found myself tied to her like a ball and chain.

Now, when it says FALSE WORDS, what does that mean? Does it mean that the words used by themselves are false? I really want you to get this, **because nobody is going to exploit you with unbiblical words.** Words only have value, either false or true, by the other words that surround them.

Tithe is a perfectly Biblical word with an application for a purpose in God's economy, but take that word and pervert it to mean something that it doesn't, like, **"You must tithe money - 10% of your gross income to your local church or you will be cursed with a curse,"** and now you are being fraudulently exploited, because you never learned some very simple truths about tithing (which is only mentioned in the gospels three times and in the book of Hebrews twice).

Now when Jesus mentioned tithing it was a REPROOF:

Matthew 23:23 NASB
"Woe to you, scribes and Pharisees, hypocrites! For you **tithe** mint and dill and cummin, **and have neglected** the weightier provisions of the law: **justice and mercy and faithfulness;** but these are the things you should have done without neglecting the others."

Look closely at the meticulous detail. He is saying, "You go out to your little herb garden on the side of your house and make sure that you carefully measure out a tenth portion of these tiny, leafy plants, but you ignore things like **JUSTICE, MERCY, AND FAITHFULNESS**, which are all detailed in **many** places in scripture."

Tithing has very little significance in the broad scriptures, but according to your lying pastor, **"If you don't tithe, God can in no way bless you financially."** But teaching faithfulness in marriage is foreign to them, because they are treacherous to the core! According to a recent study 50% of pastors' marriages will end in divorce. So, when they tell adulterers that:

"You are married in God's sight and it is sanctified and HOLY," they are again exploiting you in your ignorance with false words!

All of the words in this book are value neutral. They mean nothing until I arrange them into sentences, paragraphs and chapters. And then, chapters in successive order build upon the preceding chapters. This is how apostles build from the foundation. It is also how to properly interpret the Word of God in the context of the whole (from Genesis to Revelation). Sometimes context can be derived from the verses in the same passage, but most of the time you have to look elsewhere in order to determine a teaching's total application.

Holy Whoredom

The absolute nonsensical misuse of the Greek scriptures (N.T.), in order to bring you into bondage to the false tithe teaching is, without a doubt, one of the ways that you are being exploited by greed. Do you really want to argue with this? I can quote more verses on tithing. But is it really necessary?

Do you see how they have used this teaching to their own covetous advantage, because you were too stupid to see verses and principles that I saw when I was a new believer the very first time I read them? Did that mean that I did not give money to the church? No, I foolishly wasted my meager wages by giving them to prostitutes too - the EVIL WORKERS of the circumcision.

Now, I said all that to get you ready for...

Chapter 10
The Adulteress, and The Harlot Different, Or The Same?

Proverbs 2:10-17 NASB

For wisdom will enter your heart
And knowledge will be pleasant to your soul;
Discretion will guard you,
Understanding will watch over you,...

To deliver you from the **strange woman,**
From the adulteress who flatters with her words;
That leaves the companion of her youth
And forgets the **covenant of her God...**

I want you to start viewing adultery in a biblical sense, instead of a worldly secular sense. When Jesus says, "BUT I SAY TO YOU..." it is imperative that you undo your traditional way of thinking.

Matthew 5:32 NASB
BUT I SAY TO YOU...

> **...that everyone** who divorces his wife,
> except for the reason of unchastity,
> makes her commit adultery;
> and whoever marries a divorced woman
> commits adultery.

Now was Jesus negating adultery as the world views it? Of course not. If someone is having sex with someone other than their spouse, it is also adultery, but ANYONE CAN ACKNOWLEDGE THIS REALITY. It takes no spiritual discernment to spot that type of sinfulness.

What Jesus was doing here was connecting every scripture concerning whoring and adultery to remarriage, and to those who enter into these scripturally invalid marriages.

But people don't want to take the courageous stance that Jesus and John the Baptist were advocating, because christians think that their version of *"love"* is the sickeningly sweet syrupy sentimentality, which **they demand** that everyone else practice. So, close your candy store darlin' and take a look at what speaking the truth in love really is.

Paul was making a point here to expose the hypocrisy in the **WHOLE REBELLIOUS EARTHLY** church:

> **Romans 2:22 NASB**
> **You** (Roman Christians - this was not written to the world) who say that one should not commit **adultery**,
> do you commit **adultery**?

Of course you do, because you disobey this clear teaching and tolerate it in your pagan sex temples that you blasphemously refer to as Christ's church!

> **Romans 7:3 NASB**
> So then, if while her husband is living she is joined to another man, she shall be called an **adulteress**; but if her husband dies, she is free from the law, so that she is not an **adulteress,** though she is joined to another man.

So, all of the verses dealing with adultery in Proverbs chapters 2, 5, 6, 7, 22, 23, 27, 29, and 30, and all of the verses in the gospels and letters are speaking of, not only married women having "affairs" and harlots that walk the streets, but also re-married divorcees who attend church every time the doors open and pray and prophesy and work in the soup kitchen! But, since she is so violent against God's messengers, she will insist:

"I have done no wrong/WICKEDNESS"

...and get the Ahabs of christianity - weak and worthless pulpit puppets to agree with her. *"Yes honey, that mean old Elijah just hates women, and he will take it out on weak and helpless godly women like you because his own wife rightfully divorced him."*

I have actually been told by insensitive blasphemous christians, that they do not blame my wife for divorcing me. My wife had no scriptural justification or even any worldly reason to divorce me. She just did not want to be under my authority. When she took her vows she said she would obey me, but she would not - **just like the whore church in earthly Jerusalem will not submit to Christ's leadership.**

Proverbs 30:20 NASB

This is the way of an adulterous woman:
She eats and wipes her mouth,
And says, "I have done no wrong."

Getting a divorced and remarried woman to admit her sin is nigh impossible in most cases. This is what got John the Baptist thrown into prison and subsequently beheaded, when Herodias pimped out her daughter to give Herod, what I have to assume could only have been a full service lap dance with bonus sex acts thrown in as well. Do you really think a little pirouette and a couple of spins would have had such a profound effect on him, so that he would be willing to part with up to half of his kingdom? Get real - this was a vile sexual act of some sort that appealed to Herod's base nature. It is what carnal men are prone to do, lose their fortunes over sexual lust.

Holy Whoredom

I can't prove this ***explicitly*** from the text, but you think what you want, and I will think what the rest of scripture and all of human experience tells me. Tiger Woods may well lose half of his kingdom in a divorce settlement with Elin. How is that for prophetic irony! Now, I will simply bear down on you with the full weight of scripture on this topic:

ALL FROM NASB

1. **Proverbs 2:16 (***WISDOM, UNDERSTANDING, DISCERNMENT, AND KNOWLEDGE*) **WILL Deliver you from the strange woman, From the *(REMARRIED/DIVORCED)* adulteress who flatters with her words;**
2. **Proverbs 5:3**
   For the lips of an *(REMARRIED/DIVORCED)* **adulteress** drip honey And smoother than oil is her speech;
3. **Proverbs 5:20**
   For why should you, my son, be exhilarated with an *(MARRIED/DIVORCED)* **adulteress** And embrace the bosom of a foreigner?
4. **Proverbs 6:24**
   To keep you from **the *(REMARRIED/DIVORCED)* evil woman,** From the smooth tongue of the *(REMARRIED/DIVORCED)* **adulteress.**
5. **Proverbs 6:26**
   For on account of a *(REMARRIED/DIVORCED)* **harlot** one is reduced to a loaf of bread, And an *(REMARRIED/DIVORCED)* **adulteress** hunts for the precious life.
6. **Proverbs 7:5**
   That they may keep you from an *(REMARRIED/DIVORCED)* **adulteress,** From the foreigner who flatters with her words.
7. **Proverbs 7:10**
   And behold, a *(MARRIED/DIVORCED)* woman comes to meet him, Dressed as a **harlot** and **cunning of heart.**
8. **Proverbs 22:14**
   The mouth of an *(REMARRIED/DIVORCED)* **adulteress is a deep pit; He who is cursed of the LORD will fall into it.**
9. **Proverbs 23:27**
   A *(REMARRIED/DIVORCED)* **harlot** is a **deep pit**...an **adulterous** woman is a narrow well.

10. **Proverbs 27:13**
    Take his garment when he becomes surety for a stranger; And for a *(REMARRIED/DIVORCED)* **adulterous** woman hold him in pledge.
11. **Proverbs 29:3**
    A man who loves wisdom makes his father glad, But he who keeps company with *(REMARRIED/DIVORCED)* **harlot**s wastes his wealth.
12. **Mark 10:11**
    And He said to them, " Whoever divorces his wife and **marries** another woman commits **adultery against her** *(his wife)*;
13. **Mark 10:12**
    and if she herself divorces her husband and **marries** another man, she is **committing adultery** *(against her husband - added but implied)."*
14. **Luke 16:18**
    Everyone who divorces his wife and **marries** another commits **adultery**, *(again, against someone else - the covenant spouse you married first)* and he who marries one who is divorced from a husband commits **adultery** *(again, against someone else - the covenant spouse you married first)*.
15. **1 Corinthians 6**
    9Or do you not know that the unrighteous will not inherit the kingdom of God? Do not be deceived; neither **fornicators**, nor idolaters, nor *(REMARRIED/DIVORCED)* **adulterers,** nor effeminate, nor homosexuals,...will inherit the kingdom of God!
16. **Hebrews 13:4**
    Marriage is to be held in honor among all, and the marriage bed is to be undefiled; for **fornicators** and *(REMARRIED/DIVORCED)* **adulterers** God will judge.
17. **James 2:11**
    For He who said, " DO NOT COMMIT *(REMARITAL)* **ADULTERY,**" also said, " DO NOT COMMIT MURDER." Now if you do not commit **adultery**, but do commit murder, you have become a transgressor of the law.
18. **2 Peter 2:14**
    having eyes **full of** *(REMARITAL)* **adultery** that never cease from sin, enticing unstable souls, having a heart trained in greed, accursed children...

19. **Revelation 2:22**
'Behold, I will throw her on a bed *of sickness* - **("sickness" is not in original text - added by evil scribes),** and those who commit *(REMARITAL)* **adultery** with her into great tribulation, unless they repent of her deeds.

What you need to do, is apply all of these verses to divorced and remarried people, because that's what Jesus does in His blanket pronouncements in Luke 16 and Mark 10, without the betrothal exception (which doesn't apply to American Gentiles). Not a very flattering picture of your *"godly"* christian friends, is it?

No, they are not godly, and neither are you, if you avoid telling them out of fear of losing their friendship. God frowns on cowardice and shrinking back. The first occupants listed in the lake of fire are the COWARDLY and unbelieving! STOP BEING A LITTLE CHICKENSHIT AND SPEAK UP AGAINST LAWLESSNESS IN THE CHURCH. Get yourself kicked out and collect your approval from Christ.

There is a passage in 1 Thessalonians that is so often overlooked, because it is never spoken of in the context of remarriage. I hope you understand that it applies equally AND ALMOST EXCLUSIVELY to remarriage situations.

A little back story first. I had a person (Vincent) make the following bold claim on a christian website, where I was debating this MDR topic. A woman there (Cathy), by her own admission, was divorced and remarried, while claiming that Jesus was her Lord. I called her an adulteress and Jezebel. This is the same Cathy who told me to fuck off and die as directed by her true lord Baal.

Well, Vincent called me truly wicked, and clueless. Mr. christian idiot (Vincent) said:

Jesus' statement about marriage and divorce applies equally to single people having sex with different partners. Not only is it the same in principle, but single people having sex do become one flesh with whoever they sleep just the same as those who say "I do."

Well, that certainly has an appearance of sound reasoning. I mean it's just illicit sex, right? Just two people copulating, as long as it is a heterosexual romp in the hay, God views it identically the same way as adultery. But, if it should involve something perverse or unnatural, like butt sex or a sausage 69 between two men, or sex with a goat **AND** a chicken, *only then* does God raise the level of His indignation by calling it an abomination.

YEAH....that makes perfect sense. Thank you kind stranger, for setting me straight! **Well, that isn't what I said, here is what I said in reply:**
NO! It is not "equal." Add to the sexual transgression against God and the 2 involved, the sin being committed AGAINST the covenant spouse:

Mark 10:11 NASB
Whoever divorces his wife
and marries another woman
commits adultery <u>AGAINST HER</u>...

No, it is you who is clueless my sad little pretender, because God takes particular measures in retribution for adultery...or
HAVE YOU not read?

1 Thessalonians 4:3-6 NLT
<u>God's will</u> is for you to be <u>holy</u>, so <u>stay away from **all sexual sin.**</u> Then each of you will control his own body[a] and live in holiness and honor— not in lustful passion like the pagans who do not know God and his ways. **Never harm** or cheat a Christian brother in this **matter**

(What is the "matter"? This is speaking of SEXUAL SIN including adultery, as defined by Jesus in the Gospels)

...by *<u>violating</u>* his wife,[b] for the Lord avenges all such sins, as we have **solemnly warned** you before.
  a. Or *will know how to take a wife for himself;* or *will learn to live with **his own wife**;* Greek reads *will know how to possess his own vessel.*
  b. Greek *never harm or cheat a brother in this matter.*

This passage is almost identical in substance to this verse in Proverbs 6 concerning a defrauded husband being victimized (HARMED) by another man having sex with **his wife**:

Proverbs 6 NASB

...For the woman's *(the adulteress')* **jealous husband will be furious,** and *he*...

Now, the word *He* is not capitalized in ANY TRANSLATION that I COULD FIND (demonstrating the inability of the translators to apply spiritual principles to the process), WRONGLY *implying* that the avenger is the husband. But the passage in 1 Thessalonians 4 makes it plain that God will avenge spouses defrauded by someone else screwing their mate, even if it happens to occur in an unlawful, unsanctified remarriage!

...will show no mercy when *he (again not properly capitalized)* takes revenge.

VENGEANCE IS MINE SAYS THE LORD, I WILL REPAY!!!

Now, look carefully at the words in the previous verse. God **will show no mercy** when He measures out retribution concerning adultery! God doesn't approve of sodomy or casual sex between unmarried heterosexuals, because it is not holy either, but the measure of harsh judgment is in direct correlation to it's offending nature.

When contrasted with any other type of sex, adultery has a truly wronged party. In all consensual sexual acts, the participants are willing - even between sodomites. This isn't the case when there is a blood covenant involved. There is a violation of a helpless third party. This is clearly not equal. The parties committing adultery are not only hurting themselves by transgressing God's holy ordinances, they are violating a sacred marital bond. God has additional recompense for anyone who presumptuously does this.

Christians will be surprised to receive a much more severe punishment than the perverts and pedophiles whom they condemn.

So, unlike our dear misinformed christian moron asserts, there is an entirely different principle at work that is ignored by all of Baal's prophets, because they cannot see the offense that God says that He will one day recompense and avenge Himself, on the behalf of the wronged husband! I am angry (ENRAGED ACTUALLY) BECAUSE I AM SUPPOSED TO BE. I am spiritual and not carnal, like those in the church, so I AM infuriated at their shameful hearty approval of adultery. I am only reflecting God's indignation.

The man (frank gerken - his name does not merit capitalizing), who is now having unlawful sexual intercourse with my lawful wife, will be rewarded with unimaginable terror that will be inflicted upon him by God. This will be done on my behalf and to my satisfaction.

If it doesn't occur, then God's Word cannot be trusted. But it is imperative that the righteous wait upon God and not take vengeance for themselves. I have told him (frank) that Mary is my wife. So he is aware of my position, as is my wife, who ignores the vows that she made to me 24 years ago, being the current whore that she is.

If you have read this far, you may be thinking that I am unrighteous in my attitude about this whole situation. After all, doesn't Christ tell us to forgive those who have wronged us? Of course He does. Forgiveness must be administered when one truly repents of their sin. God doesn't give the impenitent sinner absolution for their transgressions.

Repentance is not merely sorrow, nor empty acknowledgment of sinful behavior. Repentance is literally the changing of one's mind, resulting in righteous actions that correct wrongs and make restitution for the consequences of their sinful actions. I am not hostile towards my wife. I leave the door open for her to reconcile with me, which she must do, if God's burning hot anger that is abiding upon her now will ever cease.

Her shameful actions are being continually advocated by those who say they are "christians," **yet none of them have the truth, which He promised to give to those who would obey Him.**

You need to rethink your faith, and make sure that you are not taking the Lord's name <u>IN VAIN</u>.

That is really the essence of the 3rd commandment in the Decalogue:

Exodus 20 NASB

You shall not take the name of the LORD your God in **<u>VAIN</u>**,

for the LORD **will not leave him unpunished** who takes His name in **<u>VAIN</u>**.

Now I am sure, that you no doubt have heard all of the silliness surrounding the colloquial meaning of this commandment. Something along the lines of:

"Do not speak the word 'God' or 'Jesus', if you are not properly addressing Him in reverent prayer or discussing theology." or "Don't just blurt out His name as a swear word to express shock or disgust."

The sacred Name of Jehovah, or Yahweh, or even God, has people making up all kinds of goofy rules. Some orthodox Jews will not speak any of the names of God for fear of breaking this command, which is almost universally broken by christians every day of their lives.

Now, there is not anything wrong with this kind of advice. I do not advocate the frivolous use of God's name for any reason, but that is no true measure of the all encompassing reality of this command, nor the penalty for those who break it. What does it really mean to take the name of The LORD in vain - (*emptily)*? What does God want? First and foremost, He requires obedience, so taking the name of the LORD (Master) in VAIN, is to call Him Lord, yet not do as He says. Jesus illuminated this mosaic tenet, when He made this statement:

Luke 6:45-49 NASB

"The good man out of the good treasure of his heart brings forth what is good; and the evil man out of the evil treasure brings forth what is evil; for his mouth speaks from that which fills his heart.

"Why do you call Me, 'Lord, Lord,' and do not do what I say?

"Everyone who comes to Me and hears My words and acts on them, I will show you whom he is like: he is like a man building a house, who dug deep and laid a foundation on the rock; and when a flood occurred, the torrent burst against that house and could not shake it, because it had been well built. **"But the one who has heard and has not acted accordingly, is like a man who built a house on the ground without any foundation; and the torrent burst against it and immediately it collapsed, and the ruin of that house was great."**

Now, whenever someone is in rebellion to the LORD'S commands (remember, any of the 10,000), they are taking His name, without any intention to actually **keep His commands.**

Obedience to Christ is the only way one can demonstrate love for Him.

John 14:15 NASB
"If you love Me, you will keep My commandments."

There is a saying in the military - "It is easier to ask for forgiveness, than it is to ask for permission." This is the standard operating procedure for most of those in the christian world.

"Just go ahead and do as you please, cheap licentious grace, imaginary forgiveness, and the precious blood will cover your disobedience."

If you spend your life calling Him Lord, and continue in your rebellion, then **you will be recompensed for each and every time you spoke His name idly.**

Holy Whoredom

Matthew 12:36 NASB
But I tell you that **EVERY** careless word that people speak, they shall give an accounting for it in the day of judgment.

How much longer do you want to continue in your blatant disregard for His unyielding statutes concerning marriage and divorce? This is not multiple choice christianity, like you have been deceptively led to believe by your evil Bible teachers, who wrongfully tell you that you have the Holy Spirit:

"Well, God hasn't told me that my 2nd, 3rd, or even 4th marriage is adultery - the woman at the well had been married five times and Jesus didn't condemn her!"

Really? Here is the scripture as being authoritative, that you need in order to settle when deciding what "God" has or hasn't told you.

2 Peter 1:17-19 NASB

For when He received honor and glory from God the Father, such an utterance as this was made to Him by the Majestic Glory, "This is My beloved Son with whom I am well-pleased"--and **we ourselves heard this utterance** made from heaven when we were with Him on the holy mountain. So we have the

prophetic word MADE MORE SURE,
to which **YOU DO WELL TO**
PAY ATTENTION
AS TO A LAMP SHINING IN A DARK PLACE,

until until until until the day dawns and

the morning star arises in your hearts.

Now, I don't want to bust your spiritual bubble, but I am going to anyway. If you think that rebellious voice rattling around inside your head is God's, then you don't get what Peter was saying in the above passage.

PAY ATTENTION...
PAY ATTENTION...
PAY ATTENTION...

This is one of the most profoundly revelation packed moments in this entire book:
Here is the readers digest version of what Peter was referring to in Matthew 17. Jesus took Peter, James, and John on a hike to the top of a mountain one day. While they were up there, Jesus' clothes became white and shiny, and two dead saints appeared out of nowhere. To top off this great "spiritual experience," The Audible Voice Of God was heard by them. Now, you would have to assume that Peter put an overwhelming amount of importance upon this event, but look at what he said in verse 19. That this occurrence, as awesome as it had to be, carried LESS WEIGHT than the **lamp of God's Word that is shining in the darkness of your heart,** *that you are not* **now paying attention to!**

Here is a suggestion. If you *really* want to hear The Audible Voice of God to give you direction, this is all that you need to do. Read this book out loud to yourself and subsitute your name for the word *YOU* in every place that you find a reproof. Now you are hearing The Audible Voice of God that you are under commandment to obey, because I am God's Son and He very clearly instructs you to listen to me.

You have the written Word of God regarding everything that you would ever need in order to make a righteous determination concerning who is, and who is not committing adultery. Yet, you want to pick over the scriptures and **wrangle over words,** straining out your worthless **gnats and thin strands** (words/phrases) **that you have twisted together** from a handful of verses, to the exclusion of everything else concerning this topic, which, as I told you from the outset, was a kindergarten level course.

Now, if you desire to GROW UP in your faith, it is simple (not easy) for you to graduate and put on your big boy pants.

Holy Whoredom

Ephesians 4:13-32 NASB
...until we all attain to the unity of the faith, and of the knowledge of the Son of God, to a mature man, to the measure of the stature which belongs to the fullness of Christ. As a result, **we are no longer to be children, <u>tossed</u> here and there by waves and <u>carried</u> about <u>by every wind of doctrine</u>**, by the trickery of men, by craftiness in deceitful scheming; BUT SPEAKING THE TRUTH IN LOVE **we are to** grow up **in all aspects into Him** who is the head, even Christ from whom the whole body... being fitted and held together by what every joint supplies, according to the proper working of each individual part, causes the growth of the body for the building up of itself in love. So this I say, and affirm together with the Lord, **that you walk no longer just as the Gentiles also walk, in the futility of their mind,** being darkened in their understanding...

This is the place where the light of scripture (GOD'S WORD) - the lamp is shining right now because you can read it, but you are not paying attention to it, because you are:

...excluded from the life of God because of the **ignorance that is in them (YOU), because of the hardness of their (YOUR) heart;** and they, having become callous, have given themselves over to sensuality for the practice of **every kind of impurity with greediness...**

...But you did not learn Christ in this way **(NOT YET!)**, *if indeed* **you have heard Him** and have been taught in Him, just as truth is in Jesus, that, in reference to your former manner of life, you lay aside the old self, **which is being corrupted in accordance with the lusts of deceit,** and that you be renewed in the spirit of your mind, and put on the new self, which in the likeness of God has been created in...

...righteousness and holiness of the truth. Therefore, laying aside falsehood, **SPEAK TRUTH EACH ONE of you WITH HIS NEIGHBOR**, for we are members of one another.

BE ANGRY, AND yet <u>DO NOT SIN</u>; do not let the sun go down on your anger, and do not give the devil an opportunity. He who steals must steal no longer; but rather he must labor, performing with his own hands what is good, so that he will have something to share with one who has need. Let no unwholesome word proceed from your mouth, but only such a word as is good for edification according to the need of the moment, so that it will give grace to those who hear. Do not grieve the Holy Spirit of God, by whom you were sealed for the day of redemption. **Let all bitterness and wrath and anger and clamor and slander be put away from you, along with all malice.** Be kind to one another, tender-hearted, **forgiving each other, <u>just as God in Christ also has forgiven you</u>.**

Here is what I am telling you to do by the authority of Christ:

Step 1

REPENT - stop whoring, stop having unlawful intercourse with someone else's spouse, or stop having intercourse with someone other than your covenant spouse. No longer live as a "husband and wife" and end the relationship. I realize that this abomination may have produced bastard children, but that isn't their fault. You are commanded to stop sinning. You are commanded to right wrongs and reconcile, no matter how difficult the circumstances that your disobedience has produced.

Zaccheus was convicted to pay back fourfold to those whom he had wronged, and give half of his goods to the poor. Only THEN did the Lord say that salvation had come to his house. This is the **FRUIT of true repentance,** as evidenced by an affirming example in scripture.

Step 2

If you have wronged or defrauded anyone by taking them to court and divorcing them, then ask for their forgiveness, seek immediate reconciliation, and offer any restitution that they ask of you. I am telling you that one day it will be paid, so you may as well do it now, instead of letting it continue to store up against you.

These final two steps are for *everyone, anyone, and whosoever* calls Him Lord, so that you will no longer be taking His Name in vain, at least in this area.

Step 3

TELL YOUR WHORING CHRISTIAN ASSOCIATES TO REPENT IN THE SAME MANNER AS I HAVE OUTLINED ABOVE.

AND Step 4

IF THEY DO NOT LISTEN AND OBEY CHRIST, THEN WITHDRAW FROM THEM WITHOUT HESITATION!

Chapter 11
Putting a Pin in It

1 Peter 3:8

"To sum up..."

I could easily write another 200-300 pages, but what good would it do? Are you ashamed now? Because if you are not ashamed of the wicked fruit that you have been bearing **lo these many years (Luke 15:29)**, then I am under no obligation to reveal any deep secrets of the mysteries of God's kingdom.

This is a rather lengthy passage, but I couldn't quote any less in good conscience, and you need to read and begin to obey it immediately. It took Peter over twenty years in his own walk with Christ to come to the words he penned below. He was in bondage to sin and the lies of the circumcision himself for many years after the day of Pentecost.

1 Peter 3:1-17 NASB
Godly Living

In the same way, **you wives,** be **submissive** to your own (lawful covenant, believing or unbelieving) husbands so that **EVEN IF** any of them are **disobedient to the word,** they may be won **without a word** (THIS MEANS SHUT YOUR PIE HOLE!) by **the behavior of their wives,** as they observe your chaste and **respectful behavior.** Your adornment must not be merely external--braiding the hair, and wearing gold jewelry, or putting on dresses; 4but let it be the **hidden person of the heart...**

Holy Whoredom

There is an entire person of the Kingdom of God that is invisible - head, shoulders, knees and toes...knees and toes, and eyes, and ears, and mouth and nose...!

...with the imperishable quality of a gentle and quiet spirit, **which is precious in the sight of God.** For in this way in former times the holy women also, who hoped in God, used to adorn themselves, **being submissive to their own husbands;** just as Sarah obeyed Abraham, **calling him lord,** and you have become her children **(ONLY) IF YOU do what is right** without being frightened by any fear.

In case you want to accuse me of misogyny, I have stern warnings for the men...

...You husbands in the same way, live with your wives...

(no matter how wicked and shamefully they behave toward you)

...in an understanding way, as with **someone weaker**, since she is a woman; and show her honor as a fellow heir of the grace of life, so that your prayers will not be hindered.

To sum up, all of you (married) be harmonious, sympathetic, brotherly, kindhearted, and humble in spirit; not returning evil for evil... (by taking your spouse to court and divorcing them for ANY REASON)

...or insult for insult, but giving a blessing instead; for you were called for the very purpose that you might inherit a blessing.

For, "the one who desires life, to love and see good days, must keep his tongue from evil and his lips from speaking deceit. "**he must turn away from evil and do good**; he must seek peace and pursue it. "for the eyes of the lord are **toward the righteous**, and his ears attend to their prayer, **but the face of the Lord is against those who do evil."** Who is there to harm you if you **prove zealous** for what is good?

But **even if you should suffer for the sake of righteousness**, you are blessed and do not fear their intimidation, and do not be troubled, but sanctify Christ as Lord **in your hearts**, always being ready to make a defense to everyone who asks you to give an account for the hope that is in you, yet with gentleness and reverence; and keep a good conscience so that in the thing in which you are slandered, **those who revile your good behavior in Christ will be put to shame.**

For it is better, if God should will it so, that you **suffer for doing what is right** rather than for doing what is wrong.

If you think that I am in disobedience in any way, based on your carnal understanding of kindness, love, gentleness, and reverence, then will you please school me in the manner in which I am supposed to do the following:

Ezekiel 43:10-11 NASB

"As for you, son of man,
describe the temple to the house of Israel,
that they may be ASHAMED
of their iniquities;
and let them measure the plan.
"**IF** they are **ASHAMED**
of all that they have done,**
make known to them the design of the house,
its structure, its exits, its entrances, all its designs,
all its statutes, and all its laws
And write it in their sight,
so that they may observe its whole design
and all its statutes and do them."

OR THIS:

Ezekiel 2:3-5 NASB

Then He said to me,

"Son of man, I am sending you to the sons of Israel,
to a **rebellious people** who have rebelled against Me;
they and their fathers have transgressed against Me
to this very day. **"I am sending you to them
who are stubborn and obstinate children,**
and you shall say to them, 'Thus says the Lord GOD.'
"As for them, whether they listen or not

--for they are a rebellious house--

they will know that a prophet has been among them."

Ezekiel 3:7-9 NASB

**...yet the house of Israel will not be willing to listen to you,
since they are not willing to listen to Me.**
Surely the whole house of Israel is stubborn and obstinate.
"Behold, **I have made your face as hard as their faces
and your forehead as hard as their foreheads.**
"Like emery harder than flint I have made your forehead.
Do not be afraid of them or be dismayed before them,

though they are a rebellious house."

People are not unreceptive to pleasing platitudes that only foster wickedness. You must be confronted with the totality of your unmitigated rebellion toward God and His Son. This is...

THE STONE that the builders rejected, falling upon you and grinding you to powder.

I wish that this was easier, but this book is designed to reprove you and your **wicked abominations** that you have committed under the guise of following Christ. There is no way that I can simultaneously obey the command to reprove christian ministers and those who tear families apart by ungodly divorce, while keeping any appearance of civility.

There is just no nice way to inform someone that they are:

IN GROSS SEXUAL SIN
AN ABOMINATION
REBELLIOUS
WRETCHED
MISERABLE
POOR
BLIND
NAKED

I can tell you with a 100% degree of certainty according to God's Holy Word, that you are every bit guilty, and every bit without Christ in this world.

My hope is that it will produce the kind of godly sorrow that is an absolute necessity for repentance and entrance into God's heavenly kingdom. Do I hate you? Not even close, but these seemingly over the top insults and harsh rebukes are what is lacking from your milquetoast men-pleasing ministers of the false gospel (if they **are exploiting you with false words,** then they are **not being straightforward about the truth of the gospel**). You have been misled by **the DOGS** that you should not have trusted. But this came out of your own negligence to study the Word of God for yourself.

If I had not been diligently reading the Bible for all of those years, having something in my darkened mind for the Lord to put me in remembrance of, then I would probably be remarried today, enjoying my own unapproved whoring as well.

Holy Whoredom

God had mercy on me, even though this FEELS nothing like mercy, as the natural mind would define it. I am miserable and lonely, **my only consolation comes from my constant knowing that I am suffering for doing what is good and righteous.**

There will be a reward that I cannot fathom at the moment, but this is the nature of genuine faith... *HOPING FOR SOMETHING THAT IS UNSEEN...*

IT IS ONLY SEEN IN THE PROMISE OF THAT WHICH IS TO BE.

Bless you,
Believer X

www.ingramcontent.com/pod-product-compliance
Lightning Source LLC
Chambersburg PA
CBHW032116090426
42743CB00007B/371